Life Choices

Teaching adolescents to make positive decisions about their own lives

Phil Carradice

P·C·P
Paul Chapman
Publishing

Paul Chapman Publishing
A SAGE Publications Company
1 Oliver's Yard
55 City Road
London EC1Y 1SP

SAGE Publications Inc.
2455 Teller Road
Thousand Oaks, California 91320

SAGE Publications India Pvt Ltd.
B-42, Panchsheel Enclave
Post Box 4109
New Delhi 110 017

Commissioning Editor: George Robinson and Barbara Maines
Editorial Team: Mel Maines, Sarah Lynch, Wendy Ogden
Designer: Nick Shearn
Illustrator: Mark Ruffle

A catalogue record for this book is available from the British Library

Library of Congress Control Number 2005907005

ISBN10 1-4129-1816-2
ISBN13 978-1-4129-1816-9
ISBN10 1-4129-1817-0 (pbk)
ISBN13 978-1-4129-1817-6 (pbk)

Printed on paper from sustainable resources

Printed in Great Britain by The Cromwell Press Ltd, Trowbridge, Wiltshire

Life

Choices

A Lucky Duck Book

Contents

How to use the CD-ROM

The CD-ROM contains a PDF file labelled 'Colour illustrations.pdf' which consists of posters for each lesson in this resource. You will need Acrobat Reader version 3 or higher to view and print these resources.

The documents are set up to print to A4 but you can enlarge them to A3 by increasing the output percentage at the point of printing using the page set-up settings for your printer.

Preface

Making choices is central to the human condition. From the moment we become conscious human beings we can begin to choose how we respond and with whom we interact in the social world. The ability to choose increases through time. The individual's self-awareness, self-esteem, locus of control (that is, the ability to gain internal control) all impact upon these choices and the ways in which they are made.

The stories in this series are based around the problems and joys of living as a child and young person within the twenty first century. They highlight the essential choices that people have to make in order to survive and function in a world that can seem complex and, at times, difficult to understand.

This series consists of three books which aim to help children and young people to make the kinds of choices that will achieve the best possible outcomes. There is consequently a focus throughout on the ways in which both feelings and the brain inform behaviour and our capacity to influence and make good life choices. The intention is to encourage the listener to become aware of the differences between thinking, feeling and behaving and the ways in which they can distinguish between responses based on thoughts or feelings and the majority of responses which are based on both. The aim is to encourage them to distinguish between impulsive or well thought out responses which allow for good and positive outcomes.

The series provides a 'safe' medium, the story, in which children can both identify and reflect upon good and negative choices and the outcomes that will ensue from both. Each book is designed to target a specific age range from early years to late adolescence. There are themes that are common to all three books. These include issues such as bullying, racism, inclusion, peer pressure, grief, loss, separation and coping with change among others which are pertinent to young people's lives and experiences.

Each book contains a series of stories which include opportunities for discussion, reflection and a range of follow on and reinforcement activities. There is a focus throughout on creativity and problem-solving which can be undertaken within a climate of empathy, tolerance and mutual support. The stories in the series would fulfil many of the PSHE/Citizenship requirements. Although the primary aim of the stories is to help children to make good choices and to become good citizens, we would emphasise the importance of the stories themselves. They are not merely didactic tools. They are meant to be read or listened to and enjoyed in their own right.

Margaret Collins, Tina Rae and Phil Carradice

Introduction and Background

The ability to make choices is an essential element of the human condition. From the first moment we become conscious human beings we begin to make choices about how we respond to situations and stimuli. Equally as important, we begin to decide with whom we will interact in the social world.

This ability to make logical and rational choices increases as we grow and develop. This involves concepts such as self-awareness and the gaining of internal controls. Each individual's self-awareness and ability to sustain these vitally important internal controls will impact both upon the choices that are made and the ways in which they are then implemented.

There are many ways of looking at behaviour. Traditional behaviourists view it as a product of the environment. On the other hand the cognitive view is that behaviour is the product of person variables. The cognitive behavioural model takes the view that individual thoughts and feelings work with the environment to form a 'mutual influence system', focusing on how people respond to their interpretations of experiences rather than just the experience itself or the environment. (Kendall 1993)

Clearly, then, thoughts and emotions are related or linked. The cognitive behaviour model is based on the premise that personal problems often occur because of irrational thinking. The main cause of unwanted or undesirable behaviour is therefore the connection between thoughts and emotions. (Ronen 1997)

Cognitive and Affective Domains

In order to make effective choices in our lives we need to be aware that feelings and logical thinking inform our behaviours. The purpose behind this book is to help students become aware of the differences between well thought out choices and emotional responses – and to gain an understanding that behaviour is often a combination of both. It presents them with a wide range of options, helping them to understand the difference between well thought out reactions and impulsive ones, hopefully helping them to gain the best possible outcomes when they are faced with 'choice situations' in real life.

The medium of the short story provides students with a safe situation within which they can explore, identify and reflect upon the choices characters have made. The twelve stories are all based around the problems (and joys) of living as an adolescent in the twenty first century.

Locus of Control

The stories in this book show children and adults reacting to certain situations where they either have or do not have internal controls. Internal control comes when individuals feel that they are in control of and are responsible for their own behaviours. The issue of external controls, where an individual feels that he or she is being controlled or that their behaviours are the direct result of the behaviour of others, is also explored.

The stories contain a strong emphasis on the need to develop internal control in order to make appropriate choices that will help develop positive behaviours. The concept of living with the consequences of choices or decisions – for good or for bad – is also explored in the stories.

Emotional Literacy

The characters in these stories have to deal with a wide range of problems. They have to make choices about how they can (and, ultimately, do) respond to the situations in which they find themselves. Their choices involve and hinge upon their ability to engage both their brains and their emotions. How they manage their feelings and cope with the effects of their decisions is central to the purpose of the book.

Students are asked to reflect upon their own feelings and behaviours – through the personas of the characters involved – so that they, in turn, can successfully recognise and work with the wide range of problems and dilemmas that they face each day. Surviving in a world that can, sometimes, seem increasingly hostile and unwelcoming requires significant emotional sophistication.

Peter Sharp (2001) suggests four main reasons why emotional literacy should be promoted in children:

1. We need to recognise our emotions in order to label and define them.

2. We need to understand our emotions in order to become effective learners.

3. We need to manage our emotions in order to develop/sustain positive relationships.

4. We need to appropriately express emotions to develop as fully rounded people who can help both those around us and ourselves.

In order to express emotion appropriately people have to develop internal controls, using both the brain and emotion in order to make choices. Recognising and preventing impulsive responses when they are not helpful is part of the concept of developing positive internal controls.

Aim of the Stories

The overall aim of the stories in this book is to help students make good choices that will affect their lives. Making these choices involves using both the brain and the emotions. The aims of this book are:

▶ to enable students to understand how thoughts, feelings and behaviours are related

▶ to encourage students to develop internal controls

▶ to enable students to reflect and develop strategies that will modify and inform behaviours

▶ to help students recognise impulsive responses and learn how to inhibit these.

▶ to help students become aware of the intentions of others

▶ to help students become aware of the responses of other people to their behaviours

▶ to assist students in becoming aware of the consequences of their actions

▶ to encourage students to identify good solutions to problems and then to make appropriate choices of action

▶ to help students develop a wide range of alternative solutions to problems

▶ to develop understanding of self, self-esteem and self-worth, including issues such as tolerance and diversity

▶ to assist students in gaining an understanding of the worth and value of other people and to develop an understanding of the validity of different positions or stances

▶ to encourage problem-solving skills.

The Story Topics

These twelve stories all involve making choices, of one sort or another. Whether they are the correct choices is another matter. The following topics have been highlighted in the stories, sometimes as a specific theme, sometimes as one of several overlapping themes or ideas that run through several of the stories:

- bullying
- friendship groups and inclusion
- vandalism
- delinquent behaviour
- disability issues
- being different
- running away from home
- race and prejudice
- cheating
- acceptance by the group
- teenage pregnancy
- alcohol abuse
- first love
- lying
- problem relatives
- getting your own back
- drug abuse
- loneliness and vulnerability
- shielding others from retribution
- the search for fame
- using others
- antisocial behaviour.

Using the Stories

There are several ways of using the stories. At the most basic level pupils can simply read them and give consideration to the issues involved. Reflection is a hugely valuable process and will take pupils outside the classroom environment, offering them ideas and concepts that may take days or weeks to come to fruition.

However, perhaps a more immediately effective way of tackling the concerns that are addressed in the stories is to read them together, as a class exercise. The stories are designed and have been written with the express purpose of being read aloud. They are intended for teachers to present, almost as a dramatic exercise, and then discuss the contents, either with the full class or on an individual basis, analysing the choices that each of the characters has to make.

There are several points in each story where the reading can be stopped and discussion around the issues – and the all-important choices that characters make – can take place. Similarly, at the end of each story there is ample opportunity to debate and discuss the events and the moral issues behind them. Some teachers might prefer to curtail all discussion until the end of the reading. It does not matter which way it is done, as long as debate or discussion does actually take place. Discussion is perhaps the most valuable of all exercises that can come out of these stories.

However, there are also a number of written exercises that can be particularly useful and these are outlined at the end of each specific story. These are, effectively, structures or formulas for pieces of creative writing. They are guidelines only and do not, in any way, preclude other pieces of creative writing – as decided by the teacher and/or pupils – emerging from the stories.

The issue of choice remains. As each story presents the characters, main or minor ones alike, with a number of choices one of the most useful tactics is to debate – either orally or in writing – the 'rightness' of the choice made. Did the character make the correct decision? What other way could they have gone?

References

Carradice, P. (1994) *Borderlines. Moral Dilemmas for Secondary Pupils*. Bristol. Lucky Duck Publishing. (Out of print.)

Kendal, P. C. (1993) Cognitive-behavioural Therapies with Youth: Guiding Theory. Current Status and Emerging Development. *Journal of Consulting and Clinical Psychology* 61 (2) 2 35-247

Sharp, P. (2001) *Nurturing Emotional Literacy: A Practical Guide for Teachers, Parents and Those in the Caring Professions*. London. David Fulton Publishers.

Ronen, T. (1997) *Cognitive Developmental Therapy with Young Children*. England. Wiley.

The Stories and Activities

Session 1: Just Being Myself

 Focus

  ▸   bullying and its effects

  ▸   leadership, for good or evil

  ▸   the desire to be included and accepted by peers

  ▸   being yourself, not what others think you should be.

Tasha ran as she had never run before. She ran until she felt her heart would burst out of her chest. She ran as if to outrun her humiliation. She had known it would never work, known all along that their hatred was too strong.

'Why not make friends with them?' her mother had said. 'Go to the dance Natasha, show them that you're no different from them.'

But that was the problem. She was different, different from all of them. They liked boys and dancing, they liked fashion and movies. She was quiet and shy and loved nothing better than to curl up with a good book. Even their tastes in music were different. They were always on about the latest 'Boy Band' – she played cello in the school orchestra.

'Playing the cello?' Diane had snorted earlier that evening. 'It's the only time you'll get to spread your legs for anyone.'

The laughter erupted, rolling like a bank of fog around the room. Tasha even joined in herself. Her face was crimson with shame but, inside, the pain was even worse, burning like a furnace. Don't let them know how you feel, she told herself. After all, you're here, trying to make an effort, just like your mother wanted. Ignore the silly comments, put up with the teasing, it doesn't mean a thing.

'I really don't know why you've come,' Diane said agressively. 'What the hell are you doing here? Nobody wants you. In fact, you just being here puts most people off. Why don't you go away and leave us all alone.'

The words and the tone were harsh but, then, Diane was the acknowledged leader of the pack. Tasha had never understood why. Diane was short, even a little dumpy, with a face that was always liable to break out in pimples and rashes. Hardly ideal leader material, Tasha thought, but leader Diane certainly was.

'Go on,' she snarled. 'Get lost.'

She turned away, dismissing Tasha from her mind. But Tasha hadn't gone. She had stayed and put up with the abuse, all the stupid comments that meant so little to them, so much to her. And for a while it was bearable. Only later did things become really bad.

'Tasha, come here,' Diane had called, smiling.

Nervously, Tasha walked across the room, wanting to believe Diane was being friendly but knowing, deep inside, that something unpleasant was coming. As she crossed the dance floor, strong hands closed suddenly around her arms and waist. She tried to struggle but it was no use, she was held as firmly as if she'd been wedged into a vice. Fear clamped hold of her heart.

'Hey, you lot,' Diane called. 'Look at this!'

A small group of boys standing nearby turned towards them. As they did so Diane swiftly whipped up Tasha's skirt and held it high above her head.

'There's a sight for you,' Diane called, laughing as her victim struggled and cried.

Finally, shame and terror burning at her face, Tasha managed to wrench herself free. As the laughter rolled around the hall she ran – out of the building, out into the cover of the night.

'Run, Tasha,' she heard Diane call. 'Run home to mummy.'

The night was dark but it was friendly – or so it seemed to Tasha. After a while she stopped running, knowing she could go no further. She slumped back against somebody's garden wall, pain and humiliation as sharp as a knife blade under her ribs, black hatred in her heart.

She hated Diane and the other girls, hated them for the senseless violence and the bullying. She hated her mother for having put her through this ordeal. But most of all she hated herself for being weak and afraid and giving everybody the response they had wanted – and expected.

No more, she thought, not after tonight. That's it. After tonight I live my own life. I don't care what Mum says, I don't need any of them.

And for a long while that was how it was. She ignored the taunts, the cat calls and the occasional fist in the back as she stood in the dinner queue. She would push down the fear and smile or look away, trying hard to treat her oppressors with the contempt they deserved.

One Saturday, just before Christmas, Tasha was sitting happily in her favourite chair, nose buried in the latest Harry Potter novel, when her mother appeared in the doorway. A dark shadow fell across the page and Tasha sighed.

'Are you busy, Tash?'

Tasha shook her head and looked up.

'I've got to go out for an hour or so,' her mother continued, 'but we still need some holly for the decorations. You wouldn't go up to the Common, would you, and see what you can find? When I was a girl we always used to get our holly from the Common – it's the best there is.'

She wandered away. Tasha fetched her coat, picked up a basket from the front hall and set off. It was cold and fresh up on the Common and for almost an hour she was happily engaged in finding and cutting the best branches of holly she could find. It wasn't exactly tiring and she was happy in her work.

Suddenly, however, Tasha was conscious of not being alone. Somebody was watching her. She spun around and found herself face to face with a grinning Diane. Four of her friends stood behind her.

'Well, well, well,' Diane drawled. 'What do we have here? A trespasser?'

'I'm not trespassing,' Tasha said, her throat dry and the words choking in her mouth. 'This isn't your property. You can't…'

'Can't what?'

Tasha's hand snaked urgently towards her pocket but Diane moved quickly and grabbed the mobile phone before Tasha's fumbling hands could find the keys. She shrugged and dropped the phone into her own pocket.

'Thanks,' she said. 'I always wanted one of these.'

Reaching forward, she smashed Tasha's basket from her hand. The branches of holly spilled out onto the earth. One of the other girls quickly ground them under her heel, the red berries squelching in a mass of ooze and blood.

'We can do what we like,' said Diane. 'This is our patch. We make the rules here. And anybody who trespasses on our territory has to pay the penalty.'

She inclined her head and Tasha found herself being dragged along the path. Soon they came to a ramshackle old barn. Diane kicked open the door and Tasha was pushed inside. There were several bales of straw arranged in a rough square, some bottles and cans of lager and a few empty sandwich packets. It was obviously a place that Diane and her friends used regularly.

'So what are we going to do with her?' asked one of the girls.

Diane flung herself down on a battered deck chair and casually lit a cigarette. She flicked the still lighted match in Tasha's direction. It hit her chest and fell, spluttering, onto the flagstone floor.

'Careful, Diane,' said the girl holding Tasha's arm. 'We don't want to start another fire. If the farmer catches us here again he'll go to the police. You know that.'

'Shut your mouth!'

Tasha watched as someone hurriedly stamped out the lighted match. Diane did not move. She's really enjoying this, thought Tasha, amazed to find that she was still capable of rational thought and judgement when the fear was bubbling like a fountain in her belly.

'It's about time you learned your lesson, dear little Tasha,' said Diane suddenly, hauling herself out of the chair and tossing away her dog end. 'Miss High and Bloody Mighty, thinks herself so superior. Well, maybe, it's about time you found out there's nothing special about you. Nothing at all.'

The last few words were hissed out, venomously. Diane was now barely a foot away and Tasha could feel tiny drops of the girl's spittle as it sprayed out onto her face. Diane's eyes blazed with danger. She reached out and grabbed Tasha by the hair, twisting the strands around her fingers.

'Oh, don't. Please.'

The fear was like something alive and breathing in Tasha's mouth, now. Tears sprang into her eyes and she knew that she was helpless, caught in Diane's power.

'Let's see how you like this.'

Suddenly, there was silence inside the old barn. Everyone was standing, as still and as frozen as statues, listening to the sounds from outside.

'Damn you girls!'

It was a man's voice, loud and angry.

'If I've told you once I've told you a hundred times, in my barn and smoking as well. Well, this is the last time. I'm going to take you lot to the police.'

'It's the farmer,' cried somebody, 'the bloody farmer. Run!'

With a thunderous grating, like pebbles turning on the sea shore in a gale, the barn door began to open. Slowly, it scraped across the old and uneven flagstones. The two girls holding Tasha let go of her arms and dived towards the darkness at the back of the barn. Tasha, unsteady and off balance, found herself staggering backwards. With a sickening thud she crashed into the door, forcing it shut again, and then fell, arms outstretched to protect herself.

She was never clear exactly what happened next. The door had an old bar for a lock, the type usually seen in films about Robin Hood and other medieval heroes. The wooden bar was held behind two iron teeth and, when in place, stretched across the door to keep it locked and secure. Except that this time there was no bar across the door, only Tasha's arm.

'Blast you girls!' shouted the farmer as the door slammed shut in his face. 'That's it. I've had enough of your nonsense.'

There was a violent bang as the farmer's body crashed into the door. Tasha heard the crack as her arm broke under the pressure. She felt no pain but watched the arm hanging uselessly in the frame. How on earth am I going to play the cello with an arm like that, she thought. And then she passed out.

It was four or five weeks, well after Christmas, before Tasha was able to return to school, her left arm held securely in plaster and a sling. It had been a bad break, according to the consultant, one of the worst he had ever seen, but there should not be any lasting damage.

'No school until I'm sure it's healed properly,' he said. 'Sorry, but you'll be bored to death soon.'

In fact Tasha had quite enjoyed her period of enforced convalescence. It meant she could lie back and enjoy her books without worrying that she ought to be doing something else. And without worrying about Diane and her cronies.

'Do I really have to go back?' she appealed to her mother over breakfast on her last day of freedom. 'You know Diane and her friends will be waiting for me.'

Her mother smiled and shook her head.

'You know you have to go, Tash. Just be yourself, it won't be so bad. You'll see.'

When she came in through the wide entrance doors to the school next day, the first person Tasha saw was Diane. She was standing with a group of girls, close to the reception office window, waiting to buy her lunch tickets. As soon as she saw Tasha her eyes lit up and she strode across the foyer, happily abandoning her position in the queue.

'Tasha, good to see you, girl. How's the arm? I've been worried about you.'

Tasha stared at her. Could she be genuine? As if in answer Diane turned towards her friends and beckoned them over.

'Come and talk to Tasha,' she said. 'You'll never believe what she did. You know the old barn up on the Common? The farmer caught us up there. Well, you know what he's like – a right pain in the butt! Anyway, Tasha only threw herself across the door to save me. Broke her arm, she did. Can you imagine that, blocking the door with her arm? I'd never have got away otherwise.'

She turned to Tasha and smiled. The warmth of that smile, Tasha thought, was worth a million broken limbs. Diane put her arm around Tasha's shoulder and squeezed.

'That's real friendship for you. Friends for life, eh, Tash?'

Tasha felt a warm glow in her belly. Friendship with Diane? It was all she had ever really wanted, friendship and acceptance. She grinned at Diane and the girls who were now clustering around, all of them seeming to talk at once. And then her mother's words came suddenly back to her – 'Just be yourself.'

In that moment everything seemed to fall neatly into place. She knew exactly what she had to do. Slowly, deliberately, she disengaged Diane's arm.

'No, Diane, not friends for life. Not friends at all, actually. I don't like you and, when I come to think about it, I never have done. God knows why I ever tried to be like you. Frankly, it just wasn't worth the effort.'

Diane stared at her, mouth open, a look of real amazement on her face. It was time for the final blow.

'Do you know something, Diane? I really don't need you. Do me a favour. Don't bother speaking to me again.'

She walked away, feeling the eyes of the other girls on her back and knowing that in some of them, at least, there was a tinge of admiration.

No, she did not need Diane. She had herself – and much more besides. Only she knew that her so-called act of friendship had been an accident. But she would keep that to herself. After all, as the man once said, knowledge is power.

Activities and Discussion

Ask the pupils to consider the public humiliation Tasha suffered in the opening part of the story. Was it right? Was it funny? Should it have been allowed to happen?

Ask the pupils to consider how they would have felt if it had happened to them, or if they had witnessed it happening to someone they knew.

Was Tasha's mother right to insist that she went to the dance? Was there ever a chance that Diane would accept Tasha? Depending on your answer to that, was Tasha right to go? Should she have known what was likely to happen or should she have refused to be frightened off and gone to the dance, regardless of how Diane reacted?

Ask pupils to consider why Diane bullied Tasha so badly. What did she hope to gain? Do you think that Diane bullied others or was her anger reserved just for Tasha? Why do bullies bully?

Diane obviously had leadership qualities. How could they have been better employed? What is the significance of having good leaders? What sort of behaviour should a leader display?

At the end of the story Tasha makes a choice. Ask pupils to consider if it was the correct choice. What were the possible consequences of her actions? If she had gone another way, perhaps accepted Diane's offer of friendship, what do you think would have happened? How would Tasha have felt? How would the other girls have treated her? Do you think they would have accepted her?

Writing

Rewrite the story from Diane's point of view. Try to describe how she felt, what she achieved from the bullying – and, in particular, how she felt when Tasha rejected her at the end of the story.

Imagine that Tasha made a different decision or choice at the end of the story. Imagine that she decided to accept Diane's offer of friendship. Write a story about what happened next.

Write a poem or a story about a bully, beginning with the phrase, 'I am waiting for you.' Try to imagine the feelings and emotions inside the bully. In particular, try to identify the moment when the bully made the conscious choice – to bully or not to bully others.

Have you ever been a victim of bullying or have you seen someone bullying others? Write it down, describing the event, like a story.

Imagine what it would be like to have no friends, to be left standing alone in the playground each breaktime. Imagine you are a new pupil, having just moved to the area. Would you feel frightened and alone? Or would you be confident, knowing that others would come to you eventually? Write your diary entries for the first three days at your new school.

Reflection

▶ What is more important, being true to yourself or being accepted by the group? Could you stand by your principles if it meant having no friends and being left out of everything?

▶ Is it better to make choices for ourselves or simply be told what to do and accept it without thinking?

▶ Has there ever been a time when you made a choice that turned out badly, when something you really wanted to do ended up with you hurting other people? Could you have made another choice? Should you have done so?

Session 2: The Visitation

Focus

▶ vandalism and its motives

▶ friendship groups

▶ having the courage to say no

▶ delinquent behaviour and its consequences.

A cold rain slanted in across the town. Standing there, already damp and cold, I could see the rain squalls moving up the hill towards me, misty blankets dropping yard by yard across the houses. I shivered and tried to burrow deeper into the shelter of the old chapel wall.

'Come on,' I muttered, 'I'll be soaked before anyone gets here at this rate.'

The rain was thin and unpleasant. Within minutes it lay like dew across the top of my rucksack. The hours ahead were going to be hard and uncomfortable.

'What a bloody morning!'

I turned at the sound of the voice. Bob had stolen up on me, unnoticed in the gloom. Like me he was wrapped in anorak and waterproofs, his rucksack weighted down with pots, pans and camping equipment. I smiled at my friend and together we squatted at the foot of the wall.

'Duke of Edinburgh Award?' he moaned. 'I should be home in bed. I was having a lovely dream when my mother woke me.'

I grinned at him.

'Twelve hours of walking ahead of you, mate. Try dreaming of that!'

He snorted and we lapsed into sullen silence. Five minutes later the other members of our party joined us. Toby and Dave were school-mates and, like us, they were currently more interested in their warm beds and morning cups of coffee than a twenty mile slog through driving rain.

'How the hell did we get into this?' wailed Toby as we trekked unhappily up the road. 'I tell you, if it doesn't stop raining soon I'm going home. You lot can do this on your own. I've got better things to do with my time. I don't need this crap.'

There was an edge to his voice. It was a touch of nastiness that was never far from the surface with Toby but, with today's rain and discomfort, it now seemed to have come bubbling over the top. There were times when I wondered how we managed to remain friends and, thinking about it now, I supposed that this camping trip would be quite likely to test the strength of our relationship.

We had always been interested in camping but, really, the type of camping we preferred consisted of long hot summers spent under canvas on the dunes of some local beach – camping that entailed chatting up female holidaymakers and turning a slow, golden brown under the blazing sun.

This expedition was something different. When one of our teachers suggested we take part in the Duke of Edinburgh Award Scheme we had agreed without much thought – after all, it would look good on the old CV when we came to apply for jobs or college. When we realised that it would include a lengthy hike, complete with overnight camp in the dead of winter, we began to have second thoughts. Once into the scheme, however, there was no turning back and so, on this bleak and freezing February morning, we turned our backs to the rain and trundled off up the road.

Within half an hour we were soaked but we slogged painfully on through the gloom. If anything it was lack of imagination rather than perseverance that kept us going. By midday I was exhausted. We stopped in a small village just off the main road and crowded into its battered bus shelter in an effort to get warm and put a little food into our bellies. Somebody had put a brick through the side panelling of the shelter and the wind drove in like a battering ram. I didn't mind. The relief from walking cut across the damp trousers and the rivers of rain that ran down the neck of my shirt. The peace was blissful.

'We should be in Conti's,' moaned Bob, staring glumly at the limp sandwich in his hand. 'That's where everybody else will be right now.'

He was right. Saturday lunchtime in Conti's Café, hands cradling cups of cappuccino, the air thick with cigarette smoke and gossip – it was our regular meeting place. That was where we made plans for the coming night: dancing at the club, lolling in the back seats of the local cinema or an ad hoc party in somebody's darkened front room. Thinking about it now I felt I could almost write poetry about its attractions.

'This is bloody stupid!' said Toby, suddenly. His voice was vicious.

He picked up a brick and began to hammer it at one of the bus shelter's unbroken panes of glass. The sound was like a drum, loud and threatening.

'Hey,' I said, 'pack it in. You'll break it.'

'So?'

Toby stared at me, his mouth sneering.

'It's not our shelter, is it? And anyway, the bloody thing's ruined as it is.'

He raised his hand again and, next second, the glass shattered, falling like tiny shards of crystal onto the grass outside. None of us moved, standing shocked and amazed by what had happened. In the house across the road a lace curtain twitched. Toby stuck his middle finger into the air and snarled. The curtain dropped back into place.

'Come on,' sighed Dave. 'Let's get moving. Sooner we're there, the sooner it's over.'

Slouching along behind Toby's tall figure I tried desperately to puzzle out what the hell was wrong with him. He had always been a bit offhand, rather hard at the edges, but this was different, altogether more dangerous. I tried to catch Bob's eye but his head was bent as he slouched along in the rain and so I just shrugged my shoulders and followed my friends up the path.

It was late in the afternoon before we arrived at our destination. It had rained solidly and darkly for each of the twenty long miles. We squelched through the village and made our way to a sheltered hollow at the far end of the beach. In the summer we often swam and dived from the rocks around this beach but now, as the rain swept in from the Atlantic, swimming was the last thing on our minds.

I was tempted to collapse onto the wet grass but Bob had other ideas.

'Let's get the tent up,' he commanded.

It was a horrible job. The tent was wet and our hands blistered and cut on the guy-ropes. Eventually, however, it was done. We ate some tinned meat, straight out of the cans, and damp biscuits, too tired even to consider a hot meal. Then we lay on our blankets and tried to sleep.

I twisted and turned in that half aware manner which sometimes comes on the edge of sleep but, for some reason, I couldn't seem to drop off. Relief from my aching limbs just would not come. I wouldn't have minded but the others seemed to be having no problems. Dave lay in the corner of the tent, snoring gently and looking for all the world like a half empty sack of potatoes. It was too dark to see Bob and Toby but the absence of noise from their direction seemed to be saying that they had also achieved that state which still eluded me.

Sighing, I unzipped the tent doorway and crawled outside. It was pitch black, only the sound of waves crashing onto the nearby beach disturbing the silence.

It was still raining. An owl hooted close by and, suddenly, our tiny tent and its sleeping occupants seemed very comforting. Quickly, I crawled back inside and thrust my legs into my sleeping bag.

'Keep still,' Bob mumbled.

I turned over and, before long, I too was asleep.

At 7.30 the following morning I stuck my nose out of the tent doorway and shivered. It was cold, as icy as a tomb, and even my damp, sticky sleeping bag seemed preferable to the chill of the day.

'What's it like out there?' asked Bob.

'Cold but at least it's dry.'

Two hours later I decided it was time to try again. I rummaged around at the bottom of my rucksack, managed to find some dry socks and emerged from the tent. Things were already happening. Dave had gone off to the village for milk while Bob and Toby were beginning to build a makeshift fire.

'Soon be warm,' Toby announced. 'Bacon and eggs for breakfast?'

I glanced uneasily at the huge pile of kindling, twigs and sticks he had built up in the middle of a long, grassy bank. The bank lay between us and the sea, protecting the hollow in which we had pitched our tent. Bacon and eggs sounded great but the means of producing such a feast didn't seem all that secure.

'Are you sure that's safe?' I said, pointing towards the growing mound of wood.

Toby stared at me as if I was the village idiot. Sadly, slowly, he shook his head and then turned back to the fire.

'Of course it's safe,' he said, voice arrogant and full of knowledge. 'It's far too wet to burn properly.'

I wondered. Toby always seemed to ooze confidence, even if the results of his expertise often didn't work out quite the way he planned. Once, high on the sloping dunes above this beach, he had shown me how to make a plate fly. He had flicked his wrist and his old enamel dish had spun out over the sea in a graceful, shallow arc. Bright sunlight made it glint and flame like precious metal as the plate swung back over the breakers and came to a gentle halt on the sand below us.

'Tempo,' Toby had declared. 'It's all about rhythm. You try.'

My effort shot away left and nearly took the head off a nearby bather. Toby fell over laughing and decided to abandon the lesson.

Now I gazed at him and frowned. He was probably right about the bank. There'd been enough rain yesterday to sink a battleship and the ground would be saturated. But even so, a knot of apprehension still lingered in my belly.

'I'm really not sure about this,' I said.

Toby sighed and drew himself up to his full height.

'It's not your problem,' he hissed. 'And besides, it's only grass. Who gives a shit about a pile of grass? It'll soon grow back.'

He glared at me, dangerously. I felt apprehension, not quite fear but something untoward and concerning, in my windpipe and dropped my eyes, ashamed at my cowardice and lack of backbone. Toby turned to Bob.

'Come on,' he said. 'Let's get started.'

Bob picked up a bottle of paraffin and poured it over the fire. Toby bent down, struck a match and the whole bank promptly exploded into flames!

'Bloody hell!' I screamed. 'Water. Quick!'

Orange streaks of flame leapt twenty feet into the air. We fell back before the heat as, crackling like a volley of rifle shots, gorse and bracken shrivelled and died in front of our eyes.

Hurriedly, Bob and I dived for our blankets and bowls of water. Toby stood, frowning, half smiling, staring at the fire. Beating frantically at the flames with my anorak, my mind was full of the carnage we had unleashed. It wasn't just the damage to the bank – what if we couldn't put out the fire? The whole village might go up. It would be a national disaster…

'Don't just stand there!' Bob screamed. 'Beat those bloody flames!'

He turned to Toby.

'And you,' he called. 'For Christ's sake help us.'

Toby shrugged, picked up a blanket and began to wave it in the general direction of the blazing grass. Busy as I was, it was easy to pick up on his distinct lack of enthusiasm for the job. By now a huge cloud of smoke had gathered above us as we worked, praying for even the faintest portion of yesterday's rain – anything to help put out the flames.

It took us half an hour before the last yellow glow finally expired and died. Gasping, exhausted, we stood back to survey the damage.

Three blankets had holes the size of frying pans in their centres. One sleeping bag and someone's anorak were charred to cinders while all three of us were coated in a clinging film of black ash. The bank, blackened and scorched to the colour of charcoal, lay like a beached and helpless whale in front of us.

'What went wrong?' asked Bob.

Toby shook his head, bemused but still with that annoying half grin on his face.

'I don't know, I don't understand. It shouldn't have done that.'

I was too tired to argue or tell him what I thought about him and his stupid ideas. The fire was out, that was all that mattered.

'What the hell's been going on?'

All three of us spun around, startled by the voice. It was Dave, forgotten in the heat of the moment but returned now from his trip to the village. We explained what had happened. Dave frowned and shook his head in disbelief.

'You're a load of bloody clowns, aren't you? Nobody in their right minds would build a fire there. Well, I'll tell you what, that cloud is like an Indian smoke signal.'

He pointed to the huge black pall that still hung above our campsite.

'You might just as well have run up a flag. The whole village is out, wondering what's been happening. The local policeman's about five minutes behind me. And I don't think he's coming to say have a nice day!'

His words were like an electric shock on our energy levels. Even Toby came alive, alarm clearly written across his features. The police! That meant retribution, something we certainly did not need.

It was the work of only moments to pack our gear and break camp. Exhaustion was gone and we set off at double pace, like a troop of commandos leaving the scene of action.

We were just climbing the hill to the south of the village when Bob grabbed my arm and pointed.

'Look,' he said.

Far below us, carefully picking his way across the beach towards our deserted campsite was the forlorn and avenging figure of the village policeman. Almost as one, we shuddered, lowered our heads and moved the pace up a gear. Swiftly we powered away from the beach and village and from the gigantic mushroom cloud that hovered above everything. Like an accusing finger it seemed to point after us, vandals leaving the scene of a dreadful crime.

We walked on, and down came the rain once more.

Activities and Discussion

Ask the pupils to consider if Toby is really a part of the group. Is there something in his attitude, not necessarily his behaviour but, rather, his state of mind, that marks him down as being different from the other boys in the story?

Did the boys in the story make the right choice about their expedition? Did they really want to go on it in the first place? If not, how easy do you think it would have been to call everything off and try again at a later date? Should they have done this? Or were they right to keep going? What would you have done in the same circumstances?

Why do you think Toby smashes the window of the bus shelter? What did he hope to gain by doing it? What should the other boys, the narrator in particular, have done at the moment of crisis? By not doing anything, what message was given to Toby – what were the boys really saying?

Why did the narrator of the story not try harder to stop Toby setting fire to the bank? Do you think he was afraid? Did he really believe that it was safe to light the fire? Or was it something to do with Toby being his friend and not wanting to offend him or hurt his feelings?

At the end of the story the village policeman comes to find out what has been happening. The boys do not wait; they run away quickly. Were they right to do this or should they have stayed and taken their punishment?

Do you think that Toby and the narrator would have remained friends after the events shown here? What about Toby and the other boys – would they have remained friends or would they have gone their separate ways?

Toby gave no thought to the consequences of his actions. He simply chose to do what he wanted, regardless of how it turned out. Do people who carry out antisocial acts give any thought to others? What would have been the effect of Toby's fire on the environment, on the people of the village, on visitors?

Writing

Imagine that the policeman had arrived half an hour earlier, before the boys could pack up and leave. What would have happened? Write it as a story, using any one of the four boys as the narrator.

Imagine you are Bob or Dave. Tell the story from their point of view. Do not change any of the events, just the viewpoint of whoever tells the story. Try to imagine how they would have viewed the events. Would it be a different viewpoint from the narrator's?

Have you ever been guilty of vandalism? Think carefully. Have you ever thrown a stone and broken a window; written your initials on a school desk? Have you vandalised something, perhaps by accident? Write it down as a story, not forgetting to talk about the consequences of your actions.

Imagine that the narrator had managed to persuade Toby not to light the fire. What do you think Toby would have done next? Tell the story.

The Visitation tells the story of an expedition, a trip away by a group of boys. Have you ever done anything even remotely similar? Perhaps you have made a trip to a pop concert or to a large town to go shopping. Perhaps you have been away on a camping trip. Tell it as a story but give it a twist – something goes wrong. Perhaps you miss your train back; perhaps you lose your money.

Reflection

- ▸ Would you have the courage to stand up against somebody who is bigger and stronger than you if you thought what they were doing was wrong?

- ▸ Which is most important, keeping a friend or doing what is right?

- ▸ Criminals rarely give any thought to the victims of their crime. Consider the effect of delinquent behaviour on innocent people. How do you think the victims of crime feel? Could you forgive someone who had assaulted you or stolen from you?

Session 3: A Beautiful Friendship

 Focus

▶ disability issues

▶ inclusion and acceptance of being different

▶ targeting difference.

Rob came into our lives one wet January day when the rain streamed like a waterfall down our classroom windows. Mr Rogers, our year tutor, had kept the whole class back from maths. And that was fine – anything to miss maths. It was the worst lesson of the week and old Tommy Taylor, the maths teacher, had to be the most unpopular teacher in the whole school.

'We've got a new boy joining the class today,' Mr Rogers declared, once everyone was seated and silence had returned to the room.

'Woopie-do!' hissed Jason in a stage whisper. 'Put out the flags.'

Everybody laughed and Mr Rogers shook his head in exasperation.

'That's exactly the type of response I'd expect from you, Jason. And it's the reason why I've asked you all to stay back here for a few minutes. This isn't just about a new admission to the school. This boy is quite special.'

He paused and stared out of the window towards the low squat buildings of St Margaret's on the far side of our playing fields.

'He's been a pupil over there, in St Margaret's, for the last couple of years.'

Mr Rogers inclined his head and we all followed his gaze. St Margaret's was the town's special school, lying right next to our much larger comprehensive. There were strong links between the two schools and several of their pupils came to us for lessons – integration they called it or something like that. Some came for just a few hours, others for the complete day. Our new boy, it seemed, was going to be with us full time.

'His name's Rob,' continued Mr Rogers. 'He's been over for a few visits and everyone seems to think he'll fit in quite well. The thing is, you need to be aware of his 'problem'. He's got a condition called Asperger's syndrome.'

'What's a spurgers syndrome when it's at home?' asked Jason.

Mr Rogers sighed.

'Not a spurgers syndrome, Jason. Asperger's. It's a form of autism. You've heard of that? Autism?'

He stared around the room. One or two heads nodded; most remained still.

'Go on then,' said Jason. 'Enlighten us. What's autism?'

Mr Rogers shrugged.

'Well, it's difficult to explain. But I'll try. It's a condition, an emotional or mental condition, where someone lives in, I suppose, a sort of fantasy world. They lose contact with reality, reality as we know it. They have difficulty seeing anybody's point of view apart from their own. There are various degrees of it. Asperger's syndrome is a fairly mild one but it's still a type of autism.'

'Just what we always wanted,' said Jason. 'A bloody nutter!'

'Jason!'

Mr Rogers' voice was harsh and loud – and that was unusual for him.

'If I hear you talking like that again you'll be on detention for a month. Understand?'

Jason grumbled into silence. Mr Rogers glared at us.

'I won't bore you with all the details. You don't need them. Let's just say that Asperger's is a behaviour problem. Rob doesn't look any different from the rest of us. It's just that some of his behaviour might seem a little unusual at first.'

'Oh yeah?' said Jason, his interest suddenly caught. 'Like what?'

Mr Rogers frowned. He was obviously having difficulty finding the right words.

'Well,' he said at last, 'he tends to take everything you say quite literally. So tell him you feel as light as a feather and he'll expect you to go floating up to the ceiling.'

Jason started to laugh but a warning look from Mr Rogers cut him off mid-giggle.

'It's all part of the fantasy world. So be aware of it and be careful what you say to him. Oh yes, one other thing, he doesn't like to be touched, not until he really gets to know you. So keep your hands to yourself.'

When Rob appeared in class after lunch he seemed quiet and a little overawed. He was tall with blond hair but his wide staring eyes, brilliantly blue and alive, held more than a hint of menace. Even at that early stage I guessed he was not someone to mess around with.

'This is Rob,' said Mr Rogers. 'Make him feel welcome.'

I suppose it was inevitable that Jason would be the first to fall foul of our new recruit. At the end of last lesson, as we gathered our books together in the library, he came bullocking up towards Rob.

'Hey man,' he called. 'What's it like over there in the nutter's school? Bet you're glad to be free and over here with us, eh?'

He put out his hand and roughly shook Rob's shoulder. I swear I never saw the blow but next second Jason was lying full length on the floor, blood trickling from the cut on his lip.

'Don't,' said Rob. 'Don't touch me.'

Jason stared up at him, then scrambled to his feet, dabbing at his lip with the back of his hand.

'You're bloody mad,' he cried. 'Mad!'

He flexed his fist and took a pace forward. Quickly I got between him and Rob.

'Leave it, Jas,' I said. 'You know what Mr Rogers said. He doesn't like to be touched.'

Jason snarled. For a second or two he considered launching himself forward and then, reluctantly, turned and walked away. 'Bloody madman,' I heard him mutter as he went out of the door. I spun around to face Rob.

'You really didn't need to do that, you know.'

He shrugged.

'I don't like people touching me.'

I nodded.

'Fair enough. But you don't want to make an enemy of Jason. Try keeping your fists to yourself, OK? I'm Tony by the way.'

I put out my hand, then remembered and hesitated. Half-heartedly I dropped the hand to my side. Rob grinned.

'It's OK, I don't mind shaking hands. My name's Rob.'

He grabbed my fist and pummelled it up and down. We walked out of school together and stood talking until his taxi arrived.

'The people in St Margaret's said I should come over here for lessons. They said that I'd be stretched more over here. I don't know why, I think I'm tall enough already.'

I laughed at his joke but then realised that he wasn't laughing. Rob stared at me.

'Did I say something funny?' he asked.

I shook my head.

'No,' I said. 'It's just me. Here's your taxi. See you tomorrow.'

He waved, climbed into the back of the car and was gone.

The next few weeks were interesting. Rob settled in quite quickly but didn't seem to make many friends. He always appeared to be a little distant, keeping himself to himself. Clearly he didn't need people in the way that most of us did. I suppose, if he made friends with anyone, it was with me. We didn't spend a lot of time together but at least he would speak to me between lessons and at breaktime.

He fell foul of the teachers a few times, notably with Tommy Taylor, the maths man. And that was surprising as Rob quickly showed himself as being really good at maths. He loved figures, could manipulate them in his head quicker than I could on my calculator.

It was just that Tommy made the mistake of setting the class an open question one day, to fill up the last two or three minutes of a lesson. It was a simple enough question – £5.50 an hour to drive a bus, how much would that be for a week? As Tommy spoke I saw Rob's eyes light up.

'Did you say £5.50, sir? I've got that much here in my pocket. Where can I go to pay?'

As the class erupted with laughter Mr Taylor turned red with anger.

'Are you trying to be funny with me, boy?' he demanded.

Of course, poor old Rob had taken him literally and really did think he could have an hour driving a bus for just £5.50. Tommy Taylor never forgave him and Rob was a marked man from that day forward.

Jason, of course, had not forgotten or forgiven either.

'Bloody crazy kid,' he snarled, staring with undisguised hatred across the room. 'He shouldn't be here in a school like this. He belongs in a nut house.'

It was inevitable that matters would come to a head. Every Friday we had PE last lesson. That particular day Rob and I happened to be last out of the changing rooms and by then the quadrangle was deserted. The wind was cold, howling demonically around the corners as we lowered our heads and ran for the warmer region of the covered playground. Ahead of us, out of the corner of my eye, I saw four figures waiting in the dim shadows and a small knot of apprehension gathered and grew in my stomach.

'Hang on, Rob,' I called.

He didn't hear and kept on running. When I caught up with him he was standing a few yards away from the waiting group and the tension was so real you could cut it with a knife.

'Hello, Rob,' said Jason.

I pulled up, panting, alongside Rob and stared at Jason and his friends. They were tall and tough and I knew we were in trouble.

'What's up, Jas?' I said.

He didn't even look at me but kept staring at Rob.

'This isn't anything to do with you, Tony. Keep your nose out. This is between me and the nutter.'

'Then perhaps you'd like to tell your friends to back off as well,' I said, trying to sound a lot more in control than I felt.

Jason shrugged. It was all the same to him – me, Rob, anyone who got in his way. Carefully, deliberately, he pointed his finger at Rob.

'Pay back time, nutter,' he said.

He took a pace forward and at that moment Tommy Taylor appeared around the corner of the yard.

'What's going on here?' he demanded.

Nobody spoke. Tommy glared at Jason and his friends.

'I told you lot to clear off ten minutes ago. You know the rules – nobody is to be down here after school finishes. It's a simple enough rule, even for you lot to understand.'

He narrowed his eyes, temper growing as the wind whipped across the playground. Tommy hated after school bus duty and we had clearly fallen into his path at the wrong time.

'Jason Hughes, you are already on your last warning. Much more of your nonsense, boy, and the Head will be kicking you out. Mark my words.'

Jason sniffed and feigned indifference. Yet you could see he was worried. He knew just how close he was to being excluded. I'd heard what his father had threatened, should that ever occur. And if Jason was dangerous, his dad made him look like a pussycat.

Tommy Taylor's eyes flickered over the group and finally came to rest on Rob.

'Oh, goodness me, look what we've got here. Our little friend from St. Margaret's.'

Rob did not speak, kept his head bowed low. The teacher pushed roughly past Jason and his friends and came to a halt in front of Rob and me. He was a tall man and his bulk seemed to suddenly block out the light. He glanced briefly in my direction.

'Tony,' he said, 'I'm surprised at you, being here with this crew. But you...'

He paused, glared at Rob and sneered.

'You? Well, I wouldn't have expected anything else. I'll tell you something, boy, you're going to find yourself back where you belong, in that so-called special school of yours, if you don't pull your socks up. And you'd better do it pretty damned quickly, too.'

He paused and I felt my heart sink. Don't say any more, I mumbled to myself, not another word. It was a forlorn hope.

'Did you hear me, boy?' Tommy stormed.

Slowly, deliberately, Rob bent over and lifted his trouser leg. Then carefully, ever so carefully, he pulled up his black school socks. Tommy Taylor turned incandescent with rage.

'What... what... why, you insolent young thug!'

If he could have reached over and hit Rob in the face I swear he would have done it then and there. The man was almost hopping from foot to foot in his temper. Behind him I saw Jason and his friends grinning, nudging each other with their elbows. They were loving it.

'Of all the cheeky, arrogant little buggers!' Tommy Taylor continued. 'You have to be the worst behaved boy I have ever seen...'

He ranted on and on, his voice rising like a banshee scream and echoing back from the roof of the covered playground. At last, however, he ground to a halt, exhausted, tired out from his tirade. Rob simply stared at the ground, totally untouched by the invective. For a few moments there was silence.

'Right, boy,' said Tommy at last.

He pulled himself up to his full height and took a deep breath.

'I'll be watching you, watching you very carefully indeed. Put just one foot wrong and I'll be down on you like a ton of bricks. Remember that. You won't get the better of me, I've got eyes in the back of my head.'

As he spoke we knew, all of us, what Rob would do next. His eyes widened and he leaned forward, staring intently at the back of Tommy's head. His finger came up and gently, easily, brushed the teacher's hair.

'I can't see them, sir,' he said.

Tommy's eyes bulged. He opened his mouth to speak but no sound came out. Nobody had ever dared to speak to him like that before, ever.

'Get out,' he managed to splutter at last. 'Get out of my sight, all of you.'

We took to our heels, dragging Rob behind us. We ran until we reached the bus stop and then fell, giggling and helpless with laughter, against the high stone wall.

'Oh my God,' panted Jason. 'That was incredible. Did you see his face? He just didn't know what to say.'

He turned towards Rob.

'You are priceless, boy, absolutely priceless.'

Rob shrugged.

'He said he had eyes in the back of his head. But he didn't. He lied.'

I looked at him, then at Jason. What had he called Rob? Priceless? It was going to be all right. I watched as Jason moved to Rob's side, arm snaking up and hovering above his shoulders. Rob stiffened and clenched his fist. Jason backed away, hurriedly.

'Fair enough,' he smiled. 'Maybe not yet. But we're going to have a lot of fun together, you and me. Anybody who can take the piss out of Tommy Taylor like that is a guaranteed friend of mine.'

Rob grinned at him, then at me. Deliberately, he held my gaze, shrugging and moving sheepishly on his heels. And then he winked. Could it be? I really didn't know but it certainly looked like it was going to be the start of a beautiful friendship.

Activities and Discussion

Ask the pupils to consider if they think the class was well prepared for the arrival of Rob? Could it have been done better? If so, how?

Asperger's syndrome and autism are difficult conditions that are hard to understand, partly because people with those conditions look the same as everyone else, they just act differently. Should they be included in society or should they be kept apart? What are the problems of inclusion – for the person with autism and for everybody else?

Think about other forms of disability and ask yourself the same question.

Why does Jason call Rob 'a nutter?' Should language like this be allowed?

Why do you think Tommy Taylor, the maths teacher, disliked Rob so much? Was it because of his response in the maths lesson or was there something else? Sometimes people cannot cope with difference – was Tommy Taylor like that? What about other people in the story, people like Jason and the narrator, how did they feel about this very different new boy

If Tommy Taylor had not appeared in the covered playground what might have happened? Would there have been a fight? If so, what might the result have been? Why did Jason suddenly change his attitude after the teacher had found the boys?

Do you think Rob knew what he was doing with Tommy Taylor or was it an instinctive response? Did he make a choice as to how to behave or did it just happen? What do you think Jason believed?

This story ends at the bus stop with Jason trying to be friends with Rob. What do you think would have happened to everyone afterwards?

Writing

Imagine you are Rob. Write a brief account of your feelings in the morning before you start your new school.

Find a book in the library that tells you about autism and one other form of disability. Using the information as the background then write one factual paragraph on each of the disabilities, giving as much useful information as you can – imagine you are writing for someone who has no knowledge whatsoever of the conditions.

Take the story of A Beautiful Friendship on one stage further. What happens the next day in school?

If the narrator had not befriended Rob what do you think might have happened that first day in the library? Start your story at the point where Jason puts his hand on Rob's shoulder.

Write a story about somebody who is different. It doesn't matter how they are different – they might be black in a group of white people, they might be old while everyone else is young. Start your story with the sentence, 'The trouble with Jerry (or Annie) was that he was different – and everybody knew it.'

Reflection

- ▶ Do you know someone who has a disability or a mental health problem? How do you treat them? Do you poke fun at them or patronise them? Remember, one person in every four will have mental health problems before they die. Things like depression, eating disorders and stress are all mental health problems.

- ▶ What do you think about the view that Asperger's syndrome is a 'difference' and only becomes a 'disability' through its negative treatment by society?

- ▶ Ask yourself a question – what is my real attitude towards people who look and act differently from me? Do I accept difference and celebrate it or do I prefer to follow the crowd?

Session 4: Borderlines

Focus

▶ running away from home

▶ not being understood

▶ not being listened to

▶ issues about race.

Judy threw her holdall onto the pavement below and gazed down. It was a good six-foot drop onto the roadway and she began to wish she had gone the long way round. Time was short, however, and she knew that she had made the right decision to cut across the park. It was only that the wall was so high.

Sighing, she eased herself over the edge and hung by her fingertips. Her feet scrabbled desperately for a hold, and then she smashed her knee into a protruding rock, lost her balance and fell heavily to the ground.

'Damn!' she cursed, rubbing her injured knee and fighting to hold back the tears.

She was surprised that her voice sounded so loud in the empty street and, feeling suddenly very lonely and afraid, looked around to see if anyone was near. She was alone.

It was cold, the early morning wind knifing through the darkness, coating her face in an icy mask. She had been cold before but never like this. It must be the time, she thought; 4.00 am, neither night nor day. The empty nothing of the morning.

'Come on,' she muttered, gazing urgently down the road. 'Where the hell are you, Lenny?'

She had met him a couple of weeks before. It was a meeting she would never forget. The disco had been utterly boring, just the same stupid patter from the DJ, the same cheap flashing lights, even the same bloody music. And, of course, the same awful boys.

Mark and Peter, Tony and the rest, they were all mates from school, boys she had known for as long as she cared to remember. They all had the same dreadful pick-up lines, words and phrases they'd heard on TV or read in magazines, sentiments she'd heard a dozen times before. They were all so immature, so cocky and awkward in their desire to impress.

It came as a shock to realise that she was actually bored. After a while she decided that the best thing she could do was to go home. She downed the last of her coke, told her amazed friends that she would see them tomorrow and, leaving them staring at her open-mouthed, headed for the door.

'Are you sick or something?' Emma called after her. 'You never leave before the end.'

'Just fed up,' Judy shrugged. 'Don't worry about me.'

At least her father would be pleased to see her home early for a change, Judy thought. She pushed past the dancers and then, suddenly, he was there in front of her.

'Dance,' he had said.

It wasn't a question or request. If Peter or Mark had spoken to her like that she'd have put them down straight away. 'Piss off,' she'd have said, or 'Grow up' – something like that.

But Lenny was different, so very, very different. He was tall; his black hair was coiled and braided, his skin smooth and fine like ebony. He was so natural, so sure of himself. And so she had walked out onto the dance floor, knowing that he would dance well: not self-conscious or without rhythm, and not hamming it up like most of the boys who came to the club. He was just confident, confident in himself and his ability. Compared to the boys she knew he was mature and experienced. And, as she had expected, he was a damned good dancer as well. The rest of the evening had passed in a haze. She had not gone home early that night after all – just like she didn't go home early for many other nights after that first, fateful meeting.

'How long have you lived here?' he asked as they sat at the bar between dances.

'All my life. Sixteen years in this silly little border town. Chepstow – what a place! So full of little people with little ideas. I've never been anywhere, never done anything in my whole life. The damned place drives me crazy.'

It had been a constant thread in all their conversations from that moment on. She had seen him often, nearly every night. On one glorious, never to be forgotten afternoon, she had even bunked off school to drive with him up into the Brecon Beacons. It had been a wonderful time, an idyllic period when all she could think about was Lenny and the love they had for each other.

At least, she thought he loved her. She certainly loved him. He had never told her how he felt but, just by his presence, by being there with her every night, it had to mean something special. Didn't it?

Unfortunately, after a while, she began to sense that Lenny was growing restless.

'I don't know what's wrong,' he shrugged in response to her question one evening when they were alone together in his car. 'Time to move on, I guess. I've probably been here long enough.'

A strange gulf seemed to open up in her chest, a sense of rising panic, which threatened to grow and overwhelm her.

'But where are you going?' she asked, somehow managing to stifle a sob. 'And what about us, you and me?'

He grinned at her and her heart lurched. How could she ever resist that smile, she asked herself?

'Well,' Lenny said, 'we did think about grape picking in the south of France. Me and the boys came here two, maybe three months ago. The job on the bridge, well that's almost done. I've always had a hankering to work abroad. So sometime in the next week or so, that's it. We're off. A couple of months in the sun should do us fine.'

'But what about us?' Judy repeated, the tide of fear and sorrow rising like bile in her throat.

'What do you mean, us?' he asked.

'What about you and me?'

He shrugged.

'You can come with us if you like. You keep telling me how boring it is here. Come with me and see a bit of the world. Come and see a bit of life.'

It had sounded so easy, the way he said it. If only she could. She went home and cried and thought about it. For hours, for days on end, she had thought about nothing else. What did she have to lose?

It was a cliché but her parents didn't understand her. They hadn't understood about Lenny for a start.

'Where does he come from?' her father had demanded. 'And how old is he?'

Judy had sighed in exasperation.

'He's twenty-two, Dad, and he comes from London. He's here for a few months, some sort of contract on the Severn Bridge…'

'London?' her father exploded. 'He's bloody English?'

Judy felt her anger rising.

'Well, not really. He's from Trinidad, originally. At least his family were…'

'Christ, do you mean he's coloured?'

'The word is black, Dad. Yes, he's black. So what?'

By now her father was raging, tiny drops of spittle spraying from his mouth as he shouted. Judy switched off. It was a trick she had developed over the years. Keep staring at him, nod in the right places, maybe even manage the odd, 'Yes, Dad.' But inside she could be anywhere – in school, in London, maybe even in the south of France.

'A wog,' her father stormed. 'A bloody native! What the hell is the world coming to? Christ, aren't Welsh boys good enough for you? I might even begin to understand you throwing yourself at an Englishman, at least they're white – but, bloody hell, a black. What the devil's wrong with you, girl?'

It would have been funny if it hadn't been so tragic. She hadn't expected such prejudice, not from her own father. Of course, she knew he was blinkered. She had often heard him in the Tennis Club on International Day, loudly proclaiming his nationality, condemning anybody who wasn't Welsh. But by then he had usually put half a dozen gin and tonics into his fat belly.

Raw, rank prejudice like this was much more evil. The fact that it was coming from her own father only made it worse. Much worse. To her friends the fact that Lenny was black did not matter at all. They got the odd strange look from people as they walked down the road – after all, just being black was unusual in a place like Chepstow. But to her friends it was no problem – at least, not to most of them.

'I don't know how you can ever bear to kiss him,' Emma sneered. 'I'm sure I couldn't.'

But with Emma it was pure jealousy. Anybody could see that she wanted Lenny for herself. It wasn't real prejudice, not like her father's instinctive hatred of another person just because of the colour of his skin. The thought of her father brought Judy's mind back to something he had said only the night before.

'It's ridiculous,' he had growled. 'She should be revising for her exams, not gallivanting off every night of the week.'

Judy had glanced across at the small, frail shape of her mother. As always she was hunched in her chair at the far side of the room. Her mother nodded.

'Your father's right, dear. You go out far too often. You do have your exams to think about.'

Exams! She was sick of exams. Every time, every argument, it always came around to exams.

'Get yourself some qualifications,' her father would say, 'then think about dancing. GCSEs, A levels, university. Then dancing, if you still want it – after you've got your degree.'

It was her father's pipe dream. Judy knew she could never manage university. Dancing was really the only thing she was any good at. Not just good, she was excellent, even if she did say so herself. Her PE teacher, Miss James, she believed in her. She'd cast her in one of the lead roles in the school production of Grease last year. And Judy had stolen the show with her performance.

'Drama College,' Miss James had said. 'That's where you should go. Or maybe a PE College – movement studies, something like that. You're wasted at academics, girl, but you've got a real talent as a performer. You should use it. Never waste a talent, Judy, that's a crime.'

Her father, of course, had scoffed. It had started with amusement but soon turned to anger.

'Over my dead body! You'll go to university. No way is any child of mine taking up something so common as dancing as a bloody career. Dancers? We used to have a name for people like that in my day.'

There it was again, that incredible bigotry and prejudice. If only she could be more like her brother, she thought. Paul was two years older than her, already coming to the end of his A level course. He was bright, articulate and clearly bound for an academic career. More importantly, he was exactly what his parents wanted.

'Goody bloody two shoes!' Judy stormed at him, time after time. 'Why don't you go out once in a while, get your nose out of those damned books?'

Paul would smile at her over the rim of his glasses, serene and unruffled. Nothing she ever said seemed to faze or upset him.

'I enjoy reading. I don't enjoy dancing. You do your thing; leave me alone to do mine. Fair enough?'

Her father loved it, of course.

'Paul's so considerate, just what a son should be.'

The glance he gave Judy was enough to convince her, as if she needed any convincing, that once again she was being pushed to the borders of her family. All her life, it seemed, she had been balancing on the edge.

'I'm on the borderlines,' she told Lenny that night. 'Always on the borderlines. I guess I'm peripheral, peripheral to everything.'

'I shouldn't worry,' Lenny retorted. 'They can probably cure it with drugs. They can cure anything these days.'

They had laughed and everything had been all right again. Now she stood, shivering with cold and apprehension, huddled into the lee of the old town wall. Where was Lenny? She looked at her watch, breath steaming in the cold night air. It was already gone 4.15.

'Come on, Lenny,' she hissed. 'Oh, please, come on.'

It wasn't just the cold. She knew that she was on the edge again, the edge of turning back. It had been such a hard decision to make. Lenny, when she told him, had seemed to accept it as natural. He had known all along which way she would jump.

'Great. We'll have some wonderful times. Just think of it, kid – cheap wine, sun, sand, tanned bodies.'

Judy had the sudden impression that he wasn't only thinking of her tanned body but it was too uncomfortable a notion to consider for long. She pushed the thought to the back of her mind and tried to concentrate on the prospect of all the good times that lay ahead.

'I bet you'll be really pleased to get away from this place at last,' Lenny said as he whirled her out onto the dance floor.

Maybe. But it wasn't all bad, Judy thought. Chepstow was at least home. It was secure and safe. It was familiar. She knew everybody and, more importantly, everybody knew her.

Then there was her mother. She would miss her mother. Mum always came up to her room and cuddled her after Dad's ranting and raving.

'He only wants the best for you, love,' she would say. 'He's only thinking of you.'

Dad couldn't help being like he was, she supposed. She didn't like him or his stupid prejudices, his bigotry and total lack of understanding, but she did love him – in spite of everything. And underneath it all she suspected that he felt the same. Perhaps in time they might even grow to tolerate each other.

And Paul? He might be a bit of a swot but he was nice. He didn't have any airs and graces and he usually covered up for her when another piece of foolishness had got her into hot water with Dad.

'Just keep your head down,' he would say. 'Do your damned GCSEs, keep the old bugger happy. Then do what you really want to do.'

It was good advice but it was advice she had chosen to ignore. Or had she? When Lenny had appeared the previous evening and told her to be ready to go next morning she had agreed without much thought.

'But why so early?' had been her only question.

'We want to catch the 9.00 am boat. It's a 4.00 am start, just make sure you're there. We can't wait if you're not.'

Now she looked at her watch again. 4.00 am? Hell, it was nearly half past now. She could do without all this waiting around. Still, it would all be worth it. Life on the road, free and easy, time to do whatever she wanted. It would be worth it.

OK, so her mum would miss her. And Paul. But what the hell, you couldn't make an omelette without cracking a few shells. She needed time and space to be herself, time and the chance to get away from the borderlines. She needed to find a place where people wouldn't stare at them just because Lenny's skin was a different colour from hers.

From the bottom of the hill a faint glow of orange light began to spread up towards her. Then came the sound of a car engine, carried on the wind. He was coming.

'Bye-bye Chepstow,' she called, theatrically, to the empty street. 'I'll see you when I see you.'

There was a sudden catch in her throat, a sob or cry that stifled there and caught like a physical lump. Her eyes stung.

The car pulled up alongside her with a screech of brakes.

'Cinderella!' called Lenny through the open driver's window. 'Your carriage awaits.'

The door swung open. Judy took a deep breath. And finally made her decision.

Activities and Discussion

Ask the pupils if they think Judy's life would have been different if she had not met Lenny at the club. Having made the decision to leave early, why did she choose to stay on after she had met him?

Did Judy consider the feelings of the rest of her family when she decided to run away? Should she have thought about them or should she have considered only herself?

Judy's father is prejudiced – against black people, against the English, against anybody who is clearly different from him. What could Judy have said to try and change his opinions? Could she have said anything? Should that have stopped her trying?

Why do you think Judy's family don't understand her? Why is her father insistent on her going to university? At the end of the day, should she have listened to him or was she right in doing what she did?

Do you think Judy actually goes with Lenny? Or does she change her mind and go back home?

Lenny is a man who moves about quite a lot – wherever he lays his hat, that's his home. Do you think Judy will be happy if she goes with him to the south of France or is she likely to be hurt and abandoned? What would you advise a friend to do in the same circumstances?

Writing

The story ends without any clear decision being made on Judy's part. Does she stay or does she go? You decide.

Write the ending of the story, either with Judy climbing into Lenny's car and heading off to France or walking away, back home to her family. Start it at the point where Lenny says, 'Cinderella! Your chariot awaits.' You may need to use some of Borderlines as background material.

A friend tells you he (or she) has been asked out by someone from a different cultural or racial background. What are the points for and what are the points against this. Make two lists. (For example: For – all people are the same, whatever their race, creed or colour; we live in a multicultural society. Against – your parents will never understand; people will stare and point.)

Imagine you are Judy. Sitting, waiting in your room on the night you leave, you write a poem about your situation – a father who doesn't understand you; you are in love with someone he dislikes. Write the poem.

Go to the library. Find out about two or three people who fought against things like racial segregation and race hatred and for black rights. Write a page on each of these people.

We all have to make choices in our lives. Imagine you are standing at a crossroads. You can take one of four roads. One leads to the big city, one to a quiet village, one to a deserted beach and the other disappears into a dark wood – you cannot see where it leads or ends. Which road do you take and why? Give reasons for your choices and describe the places that you go to, the things that you see.

Imagine that you are Judy, ten years on. Depending on what you chose to do (go or stay), give an account of your life up to that point. Is it full of regrets or has it been a glorious and happy ten years for you?

Reflection

▸ How often do you feel that nobody understands you? Is this a normal and natural part of growing up?

▸ There is an old saying 'Talk out rather than act out'. Ask yourself, is it better to discuss problems before they become too big or is it better to keep your fears and worries to yourself?

▸ Life on the road – dangerous or fun? Think of the things in its favour and then the things against it.

Session 5: Your Cheating Heart

Focus

▸ cheating – good or bad?

▸ when society says cheating is OK

▸ standards and behaviours

▸ keeping in with the 'in crowd'.

The match had not yet begun but already there was a large crowd gathered around the boundary ropes. All the school knew that this was the final match of the season and that a win for Stanmore would give them the league championship for the first time in the school's history.

'Think you'll do it?' asked Sally.

They were walking towards the pavilion, Sally, Rhys and David. The two boys were already dressed in immaculate cricket whites and everyone they passed called out good wishes for the game.

'Best of luck, Rhys,' they shouted. 'Give 'em hell.'

David felt proud and pleased to be here, alongside Rhys who was the undoubted star of the team. He knew that his own place in the side was more a matter of luck than anything else, injury having forced one of the other opening batsmen out of the reckoning. Rhys, on the other hand, was there by right. He was a great batsman and a wonderful wicket keeper.

'Of course we'll win,' said Rhys, confidently laying his arm around Sally's shoulder and pulling her tight.

'You seem very sure of yourself.'

Rhys grinned.

'Sally, believe me, one way or another we'll win.'

What on earth did he mean by that, David wondered? Then they arrived at the pavilion and preparations for the game ahead forced the question out of his mind.

In the end the match was a close-run affair. The key moment came during St Dunstan's innings. Their third wicket fell when they were still eighty runs short of their target.

'This guy who's coming in now,' said Rhys as he and the other fielders gathered together at the wicket, 'his name's Tom Johnson. I play with him in the County side. He's their star batsman. If we can get him out then the game's ours.'

Tom Johnson arrived at the wicket, nodded briefly to Rhys and took his guard. As Rhys had said he was clearly a good cricketer. The first two balls he faced were smashed wickedly through the covers for four and he flexed his shoulders as if he was preparing himself for a long innings.

'Come on,' breathed Rhys. 'Miss one. Just for me, miss one.'

It took four or five deliveries but eventually Tom Johnson played forward to a wickedly spinning ball and missed it. The ball shot past the edge of his bat on its way to the wicket keeper's gloves. The next second there was a loud click and the bails went flying off the top of the wicket.

'Howzat?' shouted Rhys.

David, standing out at square leg, could hardly believe what he had seen. As he had gathered the spinning ball, just outside the line of the stumps, Rhys had nudged the wicket with his left pad. The bails had fallen and the umpire, his view hidden by Tom's body, was not sure what had happened. Had the batsman been bowled or stumped or maybe even caught? All he could see were the bails lying on the grass and the close fielders, taking their cue from Rhys, with their arms in the air, screaming for the wicket. Hesitantly, unsure, the umpire's finger was raised. Tom Johnson was out.

Rhys glanced across at David and winked.

'More than one way to skin a cat,' he said.

'But he's not out,' David protested. 'The ball didn't hit the wicket, you did. There's no way he…'

'Shut it!'

Rhys' voice was icy. He stared at his friend and slowly padded across to face him. He stopped six inches short.

'Nobody knows that except you and me. We had to get him out, and that's exactly what we've done.'

'But it's not fair, it's not right.'

'Right? What's that got to do with anything? This is sport, boy. It happens all the time. Turn on the telly and you see it. Look at any cricket match. Or rugby or soccer game, come to that. It's called playing the ref.'

'But Rhys, it's cheating.'

David felt the colour rising to his face as Rhys glared at him. The bigger boy had taken off his wicket keeper's gloves and now he prodded David, hard, in the chest.

'What do you want me to do? Call him back? Tell the umpire I cheated? That would really make us look clever, wouldn't it?'

David knew it was a good argument. He didn't want to be the cause of getting his school kicked out of the tournament. Or of losing Rhys' friendship either. As if sensing his power Rhys smiled and patted David lightly on the cheek.

'You know it makes sense. Now let's get back to the game – people are starting to stare at us.'

He moved back to his position.

'Good lad,' he called without even looking at David.

Tom Johnson knew what had happened, of course. After the game they were sitting on the pavilion steps when he sauntered across, his tall shape suddenly blocking out the daylight.

'Clever stuff,' he said, 'that trick you got me with.'

'No hard feelings?' asked Rhys, a little apprehensively, as he struggled to his feet.

Tom shrugged.

'Not from me. All's fair in love and war – and cricket. If the umpire's daft enough to give it...'

He left the sentence unfinished and turned away. Suddenly he paused and looked back over his shoulder.

'Just don't turn your back on me next season.'

Rhys raised his hand in acknowledgement and sat down again. He was breathing a little more easily now, David noticed.

Sally soon joined them and walked with them into town. She was excited, her blue eyes sparkling and alive.

'That was a great win,' she enthused. 'Wonderful. Just what the school needed. That should really put us on the map.'

Stanmore was a new school in the area, made up from two older establishments that had recently closed. Most of the other schools in the town looked down on them, regarding the place as second rate with no history and very few worthwhile traditions. By winning the local cricket league, taking the title from other, longer established schools, they all knew they had gone a long way towards ending the snobbery.

Rhys glanced furtively across at David and smiled.

'Good job we got Tom Johnson out early then, wasn't it?'

David said nothing but followed Rhys and Sally into the café where the rest of the team were already celebrating. He did not stop long, taking the first chance he could to slip quietly away. As he went out of the door, leaving Rhys with his arm draped easily around Sally's waist, a momentary pang of envy shot through his chest. Don't be stupid, he told himself, she's Rhys' girl. You haven't got a chance there. He closed the café door and went up the hill towards his home.

The next Monday saw the start of the school mock and end of term exams. When David went into the form room that morning the first person he saw was Rhys, standing in front of the window. He was staring at a history textbook that had been propped up on the ledge, carefully copying dates onto his arm. When he had finished he stood back to survey his handiwork – his whole forearm was a mass of blue ink.

'What on earth are you doing that for?' David asked.

'Insurance,' Rhys grinned.

He slammed the book shut, patted David on the shoulder and waltzed easily out through the doorway. David stared after him, marvelling at the boy's confidence and energy.

'He doesn't need to do it, you know.'

David turned. Sally was standing behind him, smiling, her blonde hair gleaming and glistening in the morning sunlight.

'Sorry?'

'Rhys. He probably knows all those dates off by heart.'

'So why does he do it?'

Sally shrugged.

'He just loves the buzz, I guess. I don't think he even wants to do well in the exams. Not particularly. He just loves the act of cheating. He can't help it, it's just him, part of his character.'

She smiled and wandered away to the other side of the room. David thought back to the cricket match and realised that Sally was right. Rhys had got more pleasure out of cheating that one wicket than he had in winning the match – and the league.

He shrugged. Well, if Rhys wanted to cheat in the exams then it was his business. He knew the risks. He supposed that taking risks like that was all part of the boy's charm, one of the reasons girls like Sally were only too willing to fall for his chat up lines. Rhys was probably one of the most popular boys in the school. He was good at games, clever without being a swot – even the teachers liked him. Just being acknowledged as his friend gave David a warm glow and a certain position in the pecking order.

David sighed. He had ten minutes for a bit of last minute revision. He'd better make use of the time.

The final week of term saw the usual end of year trips and outings. Rhys and David contented themselves with the odd day visit, preferring to play as much cricket or tennis as possible in the more relaxed end of term atmosphere. Sally, however, was down for a two-day trip to an outdoor pursuits centre in the Welsh mountains.

'Will you miss me while I'm gone?' she asked, only half smiling.

Rhys gathered her in his arms and kissed her on the top of her head.

'Every minute, every second,' he said and ushered her onto the bus.

They stood, waving, until the bus had lurched around the corner. Then Rhys turned to the group, gleefully rubbing his hands together.

'Party tonight,' he declared. 'At my place.'

David felt an uneasy lurch in his stomach, wondering quite what Rhys meant by a party and why he had left it until Sally was out of the way. Then it was time for registration and he pushed the unpleasant notion away and headed for his form room.

When he arrived at Rhys' house that night the party was already in full swing. Judging by the noise, the loud music, the wild yells and screams, Rhys' parents had decided to evacuate the place for the night. He only hoped the neighbours would be as understanding.

Rhys met him at the door, his arm draped around the neck of a slim dark girl. David remembered seeing her at some of the cricket matches.

'Good to see you, mate. Help yourself to a drink. Oh, this is Julie, by the way. Say hello, Julie.'

Before the girl could open her mouth Rhys whisked her away into one of the other rooms. David frowned to himself. What the devil was Rhys doing? If Sally had been his girlfriend…

Stop it, he told himself. There's no future in thinking like that.

He shook his head and went off to find a drink. It was a bad evening. Try as he might he could not get the vision of Rhys and Julie out of his mind. It was stupid, it was none of his business, but he knew that Rhys was cheating again. Only this time he was cheating on Sally.

'What's wrong with you?' asked one of his friends later that evening.

David was sitting, unhappy and brooding, in the corner.

'Nothing,' he replied.

He levered himself to his feet and went out into the garden. It was a hot evening, the air languid and heavy. The smell of roses and geraniums was almost sickly in the night air. David stood, trying to block out the aroma, breathing through his mouth. Then he saw, at the bottom of the garden, two figures. They were clinging to each other, entwined and locked in an embrace so close and tight that it made the two people seem like one. Instinctively, before he could stop, David found himself striding down the path towards them.

'Cheating again, Rhys?' he called.

The shape at the end of the garden split suddenly into two. Julie spun away, turning her back and fiddling with the buttons on her blouse. Rhys glared at him.

'What the hell's your problem?' he said.

'No problem,' David replied evenly. 'I just thought you might have had a bit more honesty about you.'

Rhys glanced at Julie and inclined his head. The girl ghosted away up the path, her shape quickly lost in the gloom.

'I think it's about time you and I had a little talk,' said Rhys.

He took hold of David's arm and started to guide him to a garden bench. David shook his head and pulled his arm free.

'I don't need to talk to you, Rhys. I've just realised what a cheat you are. You cheat at sport, you cheat in school. Now you're cheating here.'

Rhys laughed.

'What? This? Christ, boy, it doesn't mean anything. It's just a bit of fun.'

'Try telling that to Sally.'

Rhys stared at him through narrowed eyes.

'You're going to tell Sally about this?'

David shook his head.

'It's none of my business…'

'Too bloody right,' Rhys interrupted. 'It's got absolutely sod all to do with you. Anyway, Sally wouldn't believe you. We all know you fancy her something rotten. You tell her about this and I'll make it look like you're just trying to cause trouble, trying to get in with her so she'll ditch me and take you instead. I can do that, you know.'

David felt his face on fire, felt the anger burning at the back of his skull. He knew that Rhys was right.

'Yes, Rhys, I know you could do that. That's the way you are.'

He shook his head again.

'Don't worry, I'm not going to tell Sally anything. I'll leave that to you – if you've got the guts.'

He paused and pulled himself up to his full height. For nearly five seconds he stared directly into Rhys' eyes. Then he sniffed and turned away.

'You're a rotten bloody cheat, Rhys. And I've just realised I don't like that. Come to think about it, I don't like the way you behave or any of the things you do, either. I don't need this.'

He gestured towards the house behind him, ablaze with light and almost rocking with the noise. Rhys started to say something in reply but David turned on his heel and walked away. He did not look back.

Walking away from the house David thought about Rhys' words. Yes, he did fancy Sally something rotten, as Rhys had so eloquently put it. This was the first time he had really acknowledged that fact, even to himself. More importantly, for the first time he knew that he was going to get her, too, not by telling tales, not by letting her know about Rhys two-timing her. No, he was going to win her properly, as she deserved.

It would take time; he knew that. But he had time. And he knew that he would do it without cheating. Things like cheating he would leave to Rhys.

He walked on and, as he did so, he began to whistle, tunelessly and happily. He was eager for the challenge.

Activities and Discussion

Rhys cheats in order to win the cricket match. When David questions him he says that all sportsmen and sportswomen do it. Is this true? Is cheating – 'playing the ref' as Rhys calls it – acceptable on the sports field? And if so, why?

David chooses not to complain about Rhys cheating in the cricket game. Ask the pupils to consider why this is. Is it because he wants to win, because he wants to be accepted by Rhys or because he doesn't want the school thrown out of the tournament? What would you have done in the same circumstances?

David comes across Rhys copying exam answers onto his arm. Yet he does not report him. Why? Is cheating in exams acceptable or is it, in David's opinion, nothing to do with him?

When David finds Rhys cheating on Sally he finally decides to do something about it. Why? Is it worse cheating on your girlfriend than it is cheating in a sports match or in a school exam? Why is there a difference? Ask yourself the question: is it more serious than the other two examples and why has David responded differently?

Should your own desires or wishes influence you in how you should respond when someone does something wrong?

Everybody cheats, every day of their lives. We all break rules. Perhaps we look up the answer to a problem when we should be finding the answer in our own heads. Perhaps we copy somebody's work and call it our own. There is nothing wrong with bending the rules. Or is there? And when does bending the rules become a criminal act? At what point should we intervene to stop someone cheating?

Writing

Imagine that David had told the umpire Rhys had cheated. What might have happened next? Tell the story.

If Tom Johnson had reacted differently to the decision in the cricket match, how do you think things would have gone? Write a one-page story about the encounter between Rhys and Tom on the pavilion steps.

If David did decide to tell Sally that Rhys has been cheating on her, how do you think she would respond? Write a short play of two scenes, one describing the encounter between Sally and David when she returns from her trip, the other showing what then happens between Sally and Rhys.

In the library find some examples of famous 'cheats' – perhaps Ben Johnson winning his gold medal after taking drugs; perhaps the Watergate affair with Richard Nixon or perhaps the story of the Piltdown Man. Write a couple of paragraphs on each.

Write three pages of Rhys' diary, one after each of the cheating incidents described in the story. Try to imagine how he would have felt after each of the encounters with David.

Reflection

> ▶ Sally says that Rhys does not need to cheat. So why does he do it? Ask yourself what you would do in the same situation.

> ▶ Sally and Rhys are only boyfriend and girlfriend. It's not as if they were man and wife. So cheating hardly matters. Is that true? Or is the real issue much deeper? Is it about betrayal of trust?

> ▶ Have you ever cheated – in a test, on the sports field or in a relationship? How did you feel afterwards? Be honest with yourself when you answer this question.

Session 6: You Were Wonderful Tonight

Focus

▶   teenage pregnancy

▶   under-age sex

▶   responsibilities and rights.

Ailsa slammed a disc into the CD player and threw herself disconsolately onto the bed. The wailing chords of Eric Clapton' guitar pulsed through the room and Ailsa felt the waves of despair overwhelm her once more.

'My darling,' Clapton sang, 'you were wonderful tonight.'

Her mother couldn't understand this sudden liking for Eric Clapton – 'that worn out old rocker' as she called him. She couldn't understand why The Darkness, Westlife and the rest had all been relegated to the back of the shelf. Or why that song, in particular, had suddenly become so special.

It was the words, the phrase 'wonderful tonight'. That's what Darren had told her, that night. That fateful, fatal night. They hadn't been doing much, just strolling along the canal bank, her and Janey wasting time on an idle summer evening. The smell from the canal, a combination of mud and rotting rubbish, had clung to their nostrils but it was summer and the evening was mild and they really didn't mind. Suddenly Darren had been there in front of them on the towpath.

'Evening girls,' he had said. 'Fancy meeting you here.'

As a chat up line it was pathetic. But, then, it was meant to be. And she fell for it, hook, line and sinker. They walked and talked, shared a joke or two and sat idly on the swings in the grubby little park next to their school. The evening seemed to float by in a golden haze.

'Fancy a drink?' Darren asked eventually.

'Not for me,' said Janey. 'I'm going home. I should have been in two hours ago.'

She glanced knowingly at Ailsa and grinned, nudging her friend with her shoulder. She knew that Darren fancied Ailsa. That fact was pretty obvious. Then she had wandered away, stealing the odd, furtive look at the two figures standing by the swings.

'Don't do anything I wouldn't do,' she called.

Her voice had echoed through the gloom and Ailsa raised her arm and laughed.

'Why didn't you stay with me?' Ailsa sighed now. 'Oh, Janey, why did you leave.'

She rolled over onto her back and gazed around the bedroom. It was so familiar, so safe. The old dolls and toys that she no longer played with were stacked along the shelf like rows of waiting soldiers. In the middle of them sat Tammy.

'You can't throw Tammy away,' her mother had said.

She had decided to have one of her 'clear outs'. It was a periodic passion of hers, a regular ditching of unwanted possessions. It was as if the ritual of going through everything, casting away all those items she had outgrown, could put her growing up into some sort of perspective. This time it had been a particularly ruthless performance, almost like a culling. Clothes, books, riding gear, everything had gone. And then they had come to Tammy.

'Oh no, not Tammy,' said her mother.

Ailsa stood with the old cloth doll in her hands. Tammy had been her friend for years, ever since she had been a little girl. She had been her companion and confidante, her comfort in times of trouble. She should have gone years ago but, somehow, Ailsa just hadn't had the heart. As if by magic the doll had always seemed to understand her. At times Ailsa could swear that Tammy even spoke. Of course it was all in her imagination but it was also part of the doll's strange fascination.

She had not looked at Tammy for months now, had thought herself far too old and big for dolls. Her hand wavered over the rubbish bin.

'You've got to let me grow up, Mum,' she had said.

'But you can't throw Tammy away,' he mother pleaded. 'Not yet. Please.'

And so she kept the doll. And all the others as well, for her mother's sake.

Now she reached over and pulled Tammy off the shelf. Grimly with a passion that was almost like hate, she stared at the doll.

'Come on, then,' she said, 'you seem to know all the answers. What am I supposed to do now?'

The doll did not reply. Her magic was gone, gone with the child Ailsa had once been. Nobody could tell her what to do any more, nobody. Oh, they might try

– her teachers, her mother – and she might even seem to obey. But nobody could tell her any more. Not now.

'Always be your own person,' Darren had said.

It had been later that night, that warm and pulsing summer's night.

'I am,' she said. 'My own person.'

They were sitting at one end of the long line of tables outside a backstreet pub. They weren't real garden tables, just rickety old wooden ones which the landlord, taking advantage of the warm weather, had put out on the pavement. Ailsa knew she was too young to be there but Darren didn't seem to care.

'Sit here,' he said. 'I'll go and get the drinks, then bring them out.'

She had felt so grown-up, so sophisticated. Darren was tall and muscular, biceps bulging out of his T-shirt. She had seen the way Janey had looked at him. She had fancied him like mad, it was blindingly obvious. But it was Ailsa that he had picked. She glowed with pleasure and with pride. Darren came back and, smiling, placed the drinks on the table. She sipped hers. It tasted bitter and stung her throat but she said nothing and glanced up into his eyes.

'Enjoying yourself?' he asked.

Ailsa nodded and giggled.

'I really shouldn't be here,' she said. 'My mum will kill me.'

That was when he had told her to be her own person. Darren was clearly his own man, a roamer and a free spirit. And to him those few words were like a creed. So he dismissed her claim to be the same.

'No, you're not, you are definitely not. Not yet. Not until you stop grovelling to them.'

He gestured vaguely over his shoulder.

'Who's them?'

'Them. Anybody in authority. Anybody who tries to tell you what to do. You'll never be your own person until you stick two fingers in the air at them. Not till you piss them all off so much they turn purple with bloody rage. Unless you start doing things for yourself, because you want to do them and not because somebody tells you to, you'll never really be your own person.'

It was a logical progression after that. A few drinks, which made her head feel light and woozy, a quiet walk as the light finally died and the warm summer night closed in around them like a blanket. Darren knew a quiet spot, an old warehouse overlooking the canal. The door was splintered and broken and, judging by the stench, the place was frequently used as a toilet. Darren laid his jacket on the floor and drew her down towards him.

'Remember,' he whispered. 'Your own person.'

His kiss was just like she imagined. He was gentle with her, after all it was her first time. Perhaps that was why she hadn't enjoyed it very much. It had been painful and over quite quickly. But Darren seemed happy enough and, at that moment, that fact alone made her feel good.

'Are you sure it was all right?' she asked.

He smiled at her and ruffled her hair.

'My darling,' he said, 'you were wonderful tonight.'

She didn't know, then, that it was a steal from Eric Clapton. It sounded good, was exactly what she wanted to hear, and that was all that mattered. The seedy warehouse, the dirty, stinking canal – none of it was important as long as he was pleased. Later, he had walked her home and at the front door had kissed her again.

'I'll see you later.'

'When?' she laughed. 'When's later?'

'Just later. I'll be around.'

That was the last time she had seen him. At first it did not matter. She basked in the envy of the other girls, their jealousy fuelled by Janey's descriptions. It was only as the days passed and Darren did not reappear that the pleasure began to fade. He had used her, had got what he had wanted and then cleared out.

'Damn him!' she cried now. 'Damn him to hell!'

Viciously, she hurled Tammy into the corner of the room, hating with every inch of her being. The doll lay there, dead eyes accusing and condemning in the same glance.

'Don't stare at me!' Ailsa shouted.

Eventually, however, she relented and went over to pick up the battered doll. She held it tightly to her chest and cried.

'Ailsa?'

Her mother tapped lightly on the door. 'Ailsa, are you all right? I thought I heard you shout.'

Ailsa quickly wiped her eyes, glanced at herself in the dressing table mirror and went to the door. Lightly, she swung it open.

'Just temper, Mum. I couldn't get one of my algebra problems to come out.'

Her mother frowned, deep lines of worry and concern etched like map contours around her eyes.

'You work too hard, Ailsa. Exams are important, I know, but they're not everything. You have to enjoy yourself sometimes. Relax a little. Why not give it a miss, just for tonight?'

Ailsa shook her head.

'Another half hour, Mum, then I'll be down.'

She closed the door on her mother's retreating back. Poor Mum. She had a terrible need for companionship. She had seen everything slip away over the past ten years. Once her husband had walked out on her, the responsibility for bringing up Ailsa and her sister had lain heavily on her shoulders. Dad's contributions had been minimal and Ailsa could not even fix on the last time she had seen him. As long as she could remember it had been just her mother, her sister Suzie and herself. Then Suzie had gone off to college and rarely came back. Now only Ailsa remained and, soon, even she would be gone.

'What have I done to her?' Ailsa asked herself, bitterly. 'This is going to kill her.'

She hadn't worried at first, thought it was just her body playing tricks again. But when she missed her second period the facts were undeniable. After a while she confided in Janey.

Her friend was shocked, supportive but suddenly distant. It was nothing obvious or deliberate, just distant. After all, Ailsa thought, she was different now.

'You're a mug, Ailsa,' Janey said. 'Couldn't you see what he was after?'

Ailsa hung her head and cried. Of course she couldn't. She had been out with so few boys, she wasn't worldly-wise like Janey.

'We've got to find him,' Janey announced. 'He's got to be told.'

Together, they had haunted the canal bank and the back streets, looking for Darren. It was a forlorn hope. There was no sign of him. Nobody knew him, nobody had the faintest idea of his whereabouts. He had gone as swiftly and as silently as a summer breeze.

'So what are you going to do?' Janey asked.

Ailsa shrugged. What could she do? Her choices were strictly limited.

'I'd get rid of it,' Janey offered. 'If it was me.'

A horror began to well up inside Ailsa. She didn't want this baby. Hell, it was the very last thing she needed, what with college and the future beckoning. But could she get rid of it? Could she kill it? Abortion. The word was so cold and callous. Could she? Should she?

It was a question she had pondered for weeks. God, how she regretted that one stupid moment of weakness. And the unfairness of it all. It washed over her, overwhelmed her like a tidal wave. Darren had had his pleasure, his bit of fun, and then vanished like a thief in the night. It was a good comparison, Ailsa thought. After all he had stolen, stolen her life. She was the one left with the unsolvable problem, she was the one left facing ruin.

'My darling, you were wonderful tonight,' sang Eric Clapton.

Those stupid, empty words. She wasn't wonderful, she was used, used and abused. Just like a child, a helpless victim. She wished with all her heart that she had stayed a child, the child her mother had always wanted her to remain.

And the germ of an idea began, at that moment, to form in her mind. A child! Children needed protection, didn't they? Mum would love it. Maybe she, Ailsa, had to grow up but the baby didn't. Not yet, not for a long time. It was going to be all right. Suddenly, clearly, she knew it would be all right. She must tell her mother, now, tonight.

Urgently, she threw open the bedroom door and moved to the top of the stairs. Speak now, she told herself, before your courage fails you.

'Mum?' she called. 'Can we talk?'

The living room door eased open and her mother appeared, framed by the light from the room behind. She was warm, friendly and comforting. Slowly Ailsa went down the stairs towards her.

Activities and Discussion

Ailsa was naïve, she should have realised that Darren was a chancer, she got everything she deserved. Do you agree with these statements or is the girl deserving of sympathy?

Darren needs to take responsibility for what he has done. Yet he cannot be found. Boys get all the pleasure; it's the girls who are left with the problem. What do you feel about this statement?

Why do you think Ailsa's mother was so reluctant to let her daughter grow up? Surely she should have let Ailsa learn a little bit more about life? Yet she chose to keep her as a little girl. Perhaps, if she had allowed her to grow up, Ailsa would not have found herself in her awful predicament. Ask yourself whose need the mother was fulfilling.

Look at the options open to Ailsa. She could have an abortion. She could have the baby adopted. She could keep it and bring it up herself. Whatever she might choose to do there will be consequences. What do you think she should do? Give reasons for your choice.

What do you feel about young people getting involved in sex at an early age? Is it right? Can it be harmful? Or do you consider it a normal and natural thing to do? Do old people make too much fuss about the subject? Or do you think that, provided you take precautions, there is nothing wrong with sex, whatever your age?

Should the age for consenting sex be raised or lowered, after all many people are now sexually active at a young age. Discuss the points for and against.

Writing

The story ends with Ailsa about to see her mother and tell her that she is pregnant. Write an account of the talk they now have. Remember that it is likely to be a very emotional encounter.

Imagine you are Ailsa. Write down your options about what you should now do and give your reasons for and against each one. When you have weighed the evidence, make a decision – what will you do?

You are Janey. One evening after leaving Ailsa's house you come face to face with Darren. What do you say to him? How does he respond? What do you do afterwards?

Write a page in Ailsa's mother's diary after she has been told the truth about what has happened to her daughter. Think what she might say, the emotions and feelings she would need to pour out onto the page.

Music is very emotive. Ailsa uses an Eric Clapton song to help her come to terms with her problem. Make a list of the songs that mean the most to you and then say why you have chosen each of them.

Reflection

▸   Think about the problems of unprotected sex – pregnancy and disease are only two of them. There are many more.

▸   At the end of the story Ailsa has found a solution to her problem. Will it work for her or are there greater difficulties looming ahead?

Session 7: Two Pints of Dark

> **Focus**
> ▸ use and abuse of alcohol
> ▸ under-age drinking
> ▸ family relationships.

I have never seen anybody drink a pint as fast as my Great Uncle Frank. He was my grandfather's brother but everybody in our family – indeed, it seemed as if everybody in the whole town – called him Uncle Frank.

I was coming to the end of my school career and beginning to feel more than a bit grown-up. So when Frank suggested a quick pint at the pub across the road I happily agreed. I didn't know if Frank had ever heard of under-age drinking or even if he knew quite how old I really was but, to be honest, it didn't matter. He had asked me out for a drink and I was going, that was all there was to it.

Alcohol had started to play an important part in my life and those of my friends. We had recently found a small, backstreet pub where the landlord was far more concerned with his takings than he was with our ages and many of our evenings were now spent in the smoky but accepting little building. Only last Saturday night I had sunk six pints and a whisky – and without throwing up afterwards. So I wasn't unduly worried about Uncle Frank's invitation. The trouble was I didn't quite realise what he meant by a 'quick' pint.

'I'll get them,' he declared, striding into the pub in front of me.

There was only one room, small and wood-lined. It doubled as both lounge and bar-room and held only a bare minimum of furniture.

'Two pints of dark, John.'

While the barman poured the drinks I gazed around the dingy room, wrinkling my nose at the layers of dust that seemed to cover all of the flat surfaces, including the few rickety chairs and the beer stained tables pushed up against the far wall.

'Thanks,' I heard Frank say as two glasses of dark, watery liquid were placed in front of us.

I picked up my drink and smiled at the only other occupant of the place, a solitary drinker who was hunched in the corner. When I glanced back, Frank's glass was already empty. Three, four seconds at the most, I reckoned.

'Your round,' he declared.

I slurped hurriedly at the dark brown liquid, trying my best not to dribble it down my chin. Frank stared at me, eyes narrowing.

'Come on, boy, you're wasting valuable drinking time.'

I nodded at him and opened my mouth wide. The beer seemed to be sticking, like water before a dam, at the back of my throat. It was all I could do to stop retching, then and there.

'I think I'll have a lager this time,' I gasped, finally setting down my glass.

Frank shook his head and pretended to frown.

'Mixing them, eh? I don't know, that's youngsters for you. Not like in our days, eh John?'

The barman grinned and refilled our glasses. It looked like it was going to be a long night.

Somehow I managed to keep up with Uncle Frank for the next pint. It was a desperate struggle, the beer gagging and cloying in my throat, but, strangely, the third one went down far more easily. I hardly tasted the alcohol and was not that far behind Frank in slamming my glass down onto the bar top.

'Another?' Frank said. It was not really a question.

I smiled at him like an idiot. This felt so right. Humanity was oozing out of every pore in my suddenly relaxed body. I could have happily spent the rest of my life standing here with Frank in this run-down, seedy little pub. All the problems of the world had faded away and the long summer holidays stretched ahead like a golden period in paradise.

Soon, however, Frank suggested that we move on. I nodded my agreement but the movement set free an uneasy feeling inside my forehead, just like the bubble in a spirit level when it's suddenly tilted. I widened my eyes, swallowed hard and tried to dispel the giddiness. I must have looked like a goldfish.

'You OK, boy?' asked Frank

'Sure, I'm fine. Let's go.'

The next hour passed in a haze. We called at the Queen's Head and at the Royal Oak, at the Albion and at the Rose and Crown. I don't remember what I drank except that by the time we reached the Clarence in the centre of town I was throwing down whiskies at a rate of knots. Even then I was still several seconds behind Uncle Frank in finishing each drink. The man must have hollow legs, I decided, in a rare and brief moment of clarity.

By now the world had assumed light fuzzy edges and, even in my drunken stupor, I knew that I was talking with a lisp. It was not an unpleasant feeling, however, and the warning alarm bells, which began to ring at the back of my skull, were quickly blown away each time Frank demanded another round.

'Tell you what,' he said at last. 'Let's call in at the Bowls Club. Your grandfather's got a match on tonight so they'll have the bar open. It's a hell of a lot cheaper there, boy. You youngsters have got to look after your money. Although, God knows, you all seem to have enough of it to throw around these days.'

I missed the edge to his statement but by now I would have agreed to anything as long as it involved more good times with Uncle Frank. But the blast of fresh air as we tumbled out of the pub's front door quickly blew away my desire for further entertainment. My head seemed to explode into little clouds of cotton wool and a strange sweetness began to rise in my chest and belly. Nevertheless, I trundled off after Frank, trying desperately to keep down the nausea.

The Bowls Club was on the other side of town, at the edge of the park. I had played there with my grandfather on several occasions – not that I was a good bowls player. I preferred the excitement of the rugby or soccer field but bowls was clearly a game of some skill. I had marked it down for future years when age and experience had caused me to be more careful with my body.

When we sauntered up the path alongside the club the bowling green was already full of white-clad figures, chatting to each other or loosening up tight muscles. Grandfather, the Club Captain, was standing on the veranda, looking important but rather flustered. The match had not begun and, when he saw us, Grandfather's eyes widened. A broad smile spread across his face.

'Frank,' he called. 'Just the man we need. We're one short, boy, Tommy Matthews hasn't turned up. It's a vital league match. You'll have to play.'

'Bugger off!' said Frank and ambled into the bar.

I followed him in, grinning at my Grandfather and wishing I had my uncle's way with words.

'Two pints and two whiskies,' Frank told the barman.

'Chasers, now, is it?' asked Grandfather, coming up behind us. 'What do you want to get the boy drunk for?'

Frank stared at his brother, and then switched his gaze to me. He smiled, mysteriously, to himself.

'He's not drunk. Not yet. Besides, he's an old hand at it. Him and his mates, drinking every week they are. Ask anyone in town, they'll tell you.'

He downed his whisky and turned back to face his brother.

'You needn't ask again, I'm not playing. I've got more important things to do. If you need somebody that badly, ask the boy here.'

Together they turned to face me. Grandfather sighed and shook his head.

'Him? You've got to be joking. Look at him, he can't even stand still, swaying about like a bloody ballerina. And that stupid idiot grin across his face. Drunk as a coot.'

Frank shrugged and turned back to his beer.

'Suit yourself. I'm not playing so it's him or nobody.'

I grinned at them, swigging happily at my glass. I think I actually fed most of the beer into my left ear but by that stage of the evening I didn't care where it went. For what seemed like an hour Grandfather glared at me. Then, at last, he pulled himself up to his full height and tapped me, dangerously, on the chest.

'I don't seem to have much choice. You'll have to play.'

I should have protested but I didn't have the energy. Besides, it would do me good to stay away from beer for a while.

'Come on,' said Grandfather. 'We're late as it is.'

We went into the changing rooms and he handed me a set of woods. I immediately dropped one, bent down to retrieve it and dropped the other three. Crawling about on my hands and knees, trying to recover the bowls, I felt sick and unsteady but, with Grandfather cajoling me, we finally managed to gather them together and stagger outside.

The far end of the green was only forty yards away but my vision was, by now, so blurred that it could have been forty miles. I followed Grandfather down the immaculate green, wending my way unsteadily between players, woods, mats and tiny white jacks.

'Keep away from the edge,' somebody called.

Too late, I veered like a schooner in a storm to the edge of the grass, to the very brink of the ditch that surrounds all bowling greens.

'Look out!'

My left foot twisted, I lost my balance and sprawled full length onto the shingle at the bottom of the ditch. Where I had fallen, the edge of the green, normally a perfect, foot deep precipice, was torn and broken.

'God forbid,' hissed Grandfather, hauling me to my feet and trying, desperately, to repair the damaged turf. 'Bloody well behave yourself. It's taken us years to build this club. We don't need idiots destroying it in two minutes flat.'

I heard Uncle Frank laughing from the veranda but could not pick out his shape in the dark shadow of the overhanging roof. Even to my stumbling, befuddled mind there seemed to be something mocking, something loud and contemptuous in his surging, ringing tones. My head was now spinning like the blades of a windmill and there was a grey shade or edge to everything. I did not know if it was evening or just my alcoholic haze.

'Right,' said Grandfather. 'You'll play number three. Get down there and centre the jack when I send it down.'

I nodded to the other members of our group and set off down the green. I thought I was going in a straight line but loud warning cries from the other lanes soon made me realise that I was wandering like a nomad over the playing surface. When I reached the far end I turned and waved to the other members of the team.

'OK, Granddad, send her down.'

The white jack curved out in a wide, slow arc, finishing up a foot or so off centre, just in front of me. I tried to focus on it but, try as I might, I could not see less than two of them. Taking a deep breath – it had suddenly become very hot – I moved towards the jack.

'Jus' leave it to me, Granddad,' I slurred. 'I'll put it in the middle. Leave it to me.'

I tried to push the jack with my foot but missed by a good six inches. After the third attempt my addled brain began to tell me that I had no hope of ever touching the ball with anything as uncoordinated as my foot. Maybe hands would be better.

'Won' be a second.'

I bent down over the jack and was suddenly, violently, humiliatingly sick – all over the green. There was a stunned silence. Everybody's eyes turned towards me as I sank limply to my knees. I had become desperately tired, my face burned and there was a loud roaring of blood in my ears.

Grandfather, at the far end, was staring in horror and disbelief. Through the noise in my head came the strident bellow of Uncle Frank's laugh. As clear as a death-knell it rolled down the green towards me in the clear evening air.

'Great shot, boy,' I heard him call. 'Great shot.'

Then I was sick again before I rolled over onto the green and finally, thankfully, passed out.

Activities and Discussion

The narrator is under-age and yet he is already a regular drinker. Is this a good thing? Is it manly and macho? Why do young people need to drink, even though it's against the law? What does it prove?

Uncle Frank clearly sets out to get the young narrator of the story as drunk as possible. Is it a deliberate act of nastiness or is there another motive lurking inside his brain? Why would he want to get somebody so ill that they throw up and become completely incapable?

Uncle Frank is a fairly dark character whose motives are not always totally clear. What does he think about young people? And what is his relationship with the narrator's grandfather really like? Could there have been a secondary motive behind Frank's behaviour?

Do you think the narrator will ever drink again after this performance? Or are the lessons learned from alcohol abuse quickly forgotten once the individual is sober again?

'It's good to get used to drinking alcohol.' 'I can handle it.' 'You need to be able to hold your drink.' 'Things always seem a lot better when I'm drunk.' 'It's not like drugs, is it?' All these statements were made by young people. Do they make sense to you? Do you agree with any of them?

If Uncle Frank had intended having a 'quick pint' and nothing more, what do you think might have happened in the future? Would the boy have carried on with his under-age drinking? Might the police have got involved? What else might have happened?

Writing

Write an account of what happens next, when Frank and his brother bring the narrator home. How will they be received by the boy's mother or father? How will they explain what has gone on?

Imagine you are the boy next morning. Write one paragraph describing how you might be feeling.

Many famous writers have produced stories and articles about the effects of alcohol, notably people like Dylan Thomas, Kingsley Amis and even William Shakespeare. Pay a visit to the library and see if you can draw up a list of authors who have written about alcohol.

Find out about the effects of too much heavy drinking. What are the potential problems, what can it do to your health and emotional wellbeing? Write a page on the topic.

An old man, dirty and carrying a half empty bottle inside a paper bag, comes along a dark alleyway. Start with a description of the alleyway, and then move on to the old man. He has a problem. What is it? How does he resolve it? Tell the story.

Reflections

▸ Have you ever drunk alcohol and did you overindulge? How did it affect you? Did you enjoy the experience? Will you do it again?

▸ Do you believe that alcohol can destroy lives as surely as drugs and cigarettes? Can it be pleasant if taken in moderation?

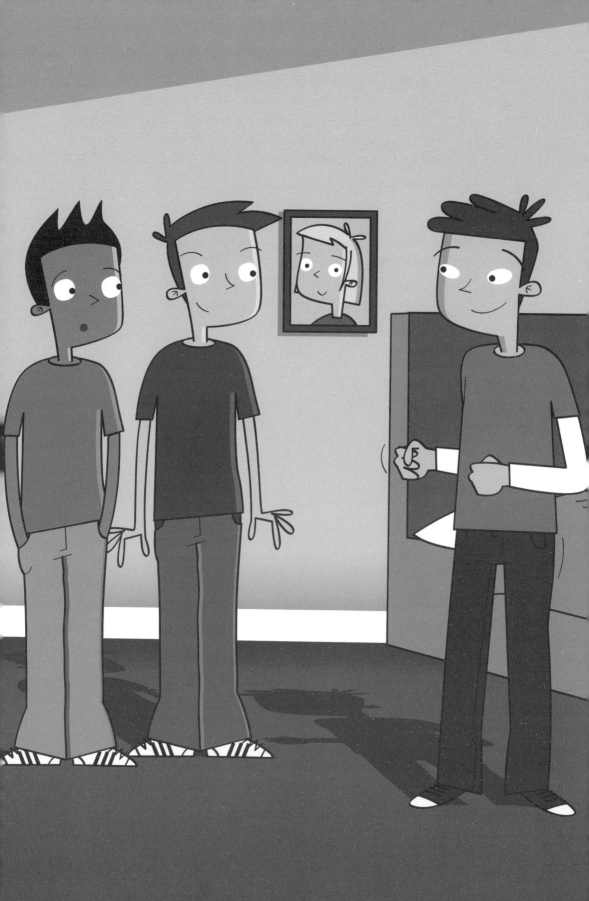

Session 8: Bearding the Dragon

> **Focus**
> ▸ first love and its effects
> ▸ telling lies
> ▸ rights of passage
> ▸ individual shallowness.

Jenny was my first love.

I was fourteen years old and, oh yes, I know what people will say. Mere infatuation, they will mumble, the first outbreak of adolescence. But for those few fabulous months it was, to me, real and glorious and vital. I had never felt such agony before and, to be frank, I don't think I have ever experienced quite the same emotion again.

The first thing I knew about it was in the school changing rooms one Saturday morning in April. We had just played our last match of the season, beating our opponents in a fast and hard fought game. I was standing in front of my locker, body tingling with the heat from the showers, fingering a bruise on my left cheek.

'Hey, what's this I hear about you and Jenny Stephens?' called Pete from across the steam filled room.

There was a shout of laughter from the other boys and from around the corner of the coat racks someone's wet towel flicked out at my bare backside.

'What the hell are you on about?' I countered, hurling a muddy football boot in the general direction of my attacker.

'It's all over the school,' Pete yelled. 'She fancies you, says she wants to go out with you. God knows why, Spotty Bloody Muldoon!'

Ignoring the laughter, I frowned at my mate Bob and busied myself packing away my muddy kit. The colour had rushed to my face but there was a strange, warm glow in my stomach.

'First thing I've heard about it,' I called over my shoulder. 'I wouldn't go out with her, anyway. She's a bloody dog.'

When Bob and I left the changing rooms a small blond boy from Year 7 was sitting on the bottom step. He jumped up when he saw us and pushed a crumpled note into my hands.

'From Jenny,' he said, nodding his head towards the girls' hockey pitch. 'No answer needed.'

I watched his thin legs hurry him away across the playground. Bob nudged me and motioned at the slip of paper.

'Better read it,' he said. 'Might be something important.'

I was embarrassed, unwilling to open the letter. But I could see the interest on Bob's face and knew that if I was too secretive all sorts of rumours would be around the school in a matter of hours. So, resigned to my fate, I ripped open the paper.

'Do you fancy a game of tennis this afternoon?' the note read. 'If you do, meet me on the old courts at 2.30. Love, Jenny.'

I shrugged.

'See? Nothing to it. She wants a game of tennis, that's all.'

Bob leered at me.

'Really? Well, if she does, it's not for your backhand drive, that's for sure. You're bloody naïve, son.'

We sauntered off to the bus stop. I was pleased, elated even. Girls hadn't bothered me much up till now. To tell the truth, they'd never seemed interested in me, always preferring handsome swaggerers like Bob and Pete. So now, to find Jenny – definitely one of the more desirable elements in the school – actually interested in me? Well, it was too much.

I was at the tennis courts by 2.15. There was no sign of Jenny and for a moment I wondered if the whole thing had been a set-up by Bob or Pete or some of the others. They would have just loved to see me standing here for an hour, fretting and worrying, while they watched, happily, from the bushes.

I looked carefully around but there was no sign of them. If they were here they were certainly well hidden. Then, suddenly, I caught sight of Jenny swinging jauntily down the road towards me. She wore a white tennis skirt, elegantly tailored and cut short enough to display her long tanned legs. I looked at my white hands and arms and at my faded denims and wished I'd had the sense to hunt out my own tennis gear. Still, it was too late now.

'Hi,' Jenny announced, opening the court gate and coming towards me. 'Glad you could make it.'

She seemed friendly but no more. I watched her pad away to the far side of the court and was puzzled. Perhaps she had just wanted a game of tennis after all.

Mind you, not that I gave her much of a game. She was a proper player, somebody who hit the ball like she wanted to kill it. I just patted the thing around whenever there were no athletics or cricket to play. She thrashed me 6-0, 6-1. Inside thirty minutes I was a quivering mess. She was as composed and beautiful as ever.

'Thanks for the game,' she said. 'You really must play more often. You could be quite good if you tried.'

I didn't reply. I couldn't. I was still gasping for breath. Jenny smiled at me and carefully placed her racquet beside the net. Her eyes sparkled as she reached out for my hand.

'Come on,' she said.

She led the way to an old air raid shelter which stood alongside the tennis courts. It had been part of an old World War Two RAF base but the military had been gone for many years now and the courts and shelters were used by the people of the town whenever they liked.

'Where are we going?' I asked.

She smiled and my solar plexus jumped ten feet. Despite my exhaustion I felt suddenly alive. Jenny was fresh and clean and there was a faint hint of perfume about her, the smell of promise – if there could ever be such a thing. It was stupid but my words from earlier that morning came rushing back to me. What had I called her? A dog? I must be mad. This girl was beautiful. She was warm and sensuous. She was like nothing I had ever experienced before.

'I want to show you something,' she said, leading the way down the steep steps into the shelter.

At the bottom we paused and she stood back against the wall. She smelt wonderful. Her scent filled that grimy old building. I could sense her, see her, touch her. My whole being was filled to overflowing with Jenny.

'Well?' she said.

'Well what?'

'Aren't you going to kiss me?'

This was it, my big moment. I had never kissed a girl before and wasn't sure what to do. I lunged forward. Three inches short she stopped me with a shake of her head.

'Gently,' she said. 'And close your eyes.'

'Why?'

'It's better that way.'

She took my head in her hands and softly, ever so softly, laid her lips against mine. The top of my brain promptly took off and somersaulted around the echoing room. I felt her hands in my hair, her salt-sweet taste like nectar on my tongue. Gaining in confidence I began to experiment. I opened my mouth, then closed it. I kissed her hard, kissed her softly, pulled back so that our lips were barely touching. A low, sensuous groan escaped from deep inside me. It was, quite simply, the greatest moment of my life.

Not much else happened that day. We played another couple of games of tennis and Jenny won six nothing both times. Quite frankly, I was lucky to get nothing. My mind was elsewhere. At five o'clock I walked her home and kissed her again at her front door. I could have spent the rest of my life just kissing her.

'See you tomorrow?' she asked.

I nodded. Tomorrow? I didn't know if I could wait that long.

'We'll go for a walk,' she said and the door closed easily on her retreating back.

The next few weeks were idyllic. We went everywhere together, on long walks by the river, to the beach, to our local fleapit of a cinema. Sometimes we just sat in Conti's Café and held hands over cups of cappuccino. I was in love for the first time in my life. Every waking moment Jenny occupied my thoughts. I could not get her out of my mind. There was a real ache in my chest when I was not with her, an all-enveloping passion when I was. And yet, for all the emotion, it was basically innocent. That, I think, was probably its greatest thrill.

Bob and Pete, for their part, were disgusted.

'Get a grip on yourself,' Pete said. 'That bloody girl's turned you into a jelly.'

I smiled quietly to myself. They just didn't understand. Nobody could understand because, apart from me, nobody had ever felt like this!

And then came the first dark cloud. One Saturday evening we were sitting in the back row of the cinema, waiting for the film to start, when Jenny sent my world tumbling.

'I'm really not looking forward to December,' she murmured.

'December?'

'When I go to live with my dad.'

I stared at her in horror.

'Didn't you know?' she asked.

Numbed, I shook my head. It was a simple enough story. Jenny's mother was dead and her father was the manager of a large department store in Manchester. She had been living for nearly ten years in our small town with her grandmother but now her father was planning to remarry and wanted Jenny to go and live with him. December was to be the fatal date.

For days on end I was heartbroken. How could life be so cruel? I lay in my bedroom, listening to my sister's maudlin Westlife records, tears only a bare few inches beneath the surface. My self-pity was all-embracing. Yet again Bob and Pete were disgusted.

'You are pathetic!' Bob snarled. 'It's only a bloody girl, for God's sake. There's plenty more of them around.'

It was Jenny herself who eventually jolted me out of my self-pity.

'Look,' she said, 'I'll miss you dreadfully. But we are only fourteen years old. We'll write, every day if you want. If anything comes of it, fine. We'll just have to wait and see. And besides, December is months away. Let's just enjoy the time we've got.'

It was sensible advice which I decided to take. I pushed all thoughts of December out of my mind and concentrated on enjoying the summer. We had a wonderful time, Jenny, Bob, Pete, all the others – and me. With beach parties, dances on Saturday nights, day trips away, the weeks went by in a golden haze.

September came and school began again. I found myself in a mad whirl of rugby matches, rehearsals for the school play and weekend dates with Jenny. I was so busy and so content that, at first, I failed to notice the subtle change in her attitude.

As October died and the wet November days spread like a grey blanket across the year, she became remote, slightly removed. Looking back, now, I can see that she was already distancing herself – from me, from the school, from our friends – ready for that looming end of term, ready for a change of life that must have been terrifying. And I was too selfish or too afraid to see it.

'I don't know why we bother going out,' she complained. 'You're always off playing rugby or training or something. I never get to see you any more.'

I suppose I had started to take her for granted. I certainly didn't try to change my way of life. Compromise was a word I had never heard. And besides, I don't think it was what she wanted.

I can't remember the cause of our final quarrel. It was probably something trivial, without sense or reason. All I know is that one evening after school, at the bus stop, we exchanged harsh words. She stormed off one way, I pouted and hurried away the other.

Strangely, what I do remember is her last comment as she whirled off down the road in a flurry of flying skirts and swirling hair. Those few brief words have lived with me ever since, burning their way deeper and deeper into my brain.

'Grow up,' she threw back over her shoulder. 'You're like a bloody three year old sometimes.'

At the time, however, I could only see things as her fault. My rage was like a living thing inside me, eating away at my reason. But I still expected to go into school next day and sort things out with her. So it came as something of a shock to find that events had overtaken me.

'Hear you and Jenny have finished,' said Bob as we huddled on the steps of the covered playground that breaktime.

I shivered but I don't think it had anything to do with the November wind. Carelessly, I shrugged. Pride would not let me do anything else.

'Yeah, I suppose so. She was getting far too clingy. Time to look for other fish.'

Bob clapped me around the shoulders.

'Good man. That's the way. Bet you had a good time with her, though?'

I grinned at him – a little forced, maybe, but a grin nonetheless. Pete, who was sitting beyond Bob, stared out onto the deserted tarmac, half-heartedly pulling on a dog-end.

'You bet,' I said. 'The best. The very best.'

I nudged Bob in the ribs and winked. Pete came suddenly alive, his eyes wide and staring. They both inched closer.

'You mean you went all the way with her?' Pete demanded. 'All the bloody way?'

A sharp pain, real and livid, shot into my chest but I could not stop the lie. Already I had gone too far.

'Of course I did. Bloody brilliant it was, too.'

They scragged me, jumping all over me, pulling my hair and punching me. But they believed me, implicitly and without question.

'You lucky bugger!' Bob hissed. 'Tell us about it.'

Shame burning at my forehead, I told them what they wanted to hear. Even then I knew it was wrong, knew it was debasing everything Jenny and I had ever had. But it was as if I was caught in a whirlwind, being dragged helplessly and heedlessly along.

Within days it was all over the school. I felt people's eyes on me wherever I went, eyes that were, strangely, full of envy and awe. Suddenly, it seemed, I had become a celebrity and, despite everything, despite the shame of my lie, despite the beauty of what Jenny and I had once experienced, I actually began to enjoy it.

That last month was a strange and evocative time. There were Christmas festivities in school, parties most Saturday nights and girls who seemed, suddenly, eager to date me. I lived life in one long daze of pleasure. And yet there was an emptiness as well, something lurking, telling me that this was all shallow and without purpose.

Several times, in school or in Conti's Café, I caught sight of Jenny staring at me. But despite a sudden tightening in the belly, I did nothing. I suppose it was pride or foolishness but invariably I just waved or looked away and we did not speak.

On the last day of term, when everyone else had gone home for the Christmas holidays, I went back to my form room to pick up some books and, in the doorway, came face to face with Jenny. She was alone and obviously taking a last look at the room.

'Hi there,' I said, glib and arrogant.

She stared at me for a few seconds, then smiled and walked past me into the corridor. I felt my heart pounding in my chest. Fool, I told myself, you bloody, bloody fool. Talk to her, now, before it's too late. I said nothing.

Suddenly, Jenny turned. She smiled again, sadly and a little wistfully.

'I'm off tomorrow,' she said. 'Take care. See you around.'

In that split second I knew, knew that she had finished our relationship to ease my pain, to make the parting easier to take.

And more than that, I knew that she knew about my lies, my bragging, empty lies. She knew and had said nothing.

Activities and Discussion

The boy in the story calls Jenny 'a dog'. Why does he do that, what is his reason for being so hard and unpleasant with his comments? Ask yourself, does he really mean what he says or is it done simply for effect? Is this, or words like it, something that young people, boys in particular, often say?

Why do you think the boy falls so hopelessly in love with Jenny? When the other boys tell him he is being foolish he ignores them because he is consumed with passion – is he right or are they? Should you get so heavily involved with someone at such a young age?

When he hears the news that Jenny is moving away the boy in the story is devastated. If he had not been so infatuated, would it have hurt so much?

Why did the narrator tell his lie about Jenny? Sometimes we get put in situations where we say things we don't really mean. It's as if events have overtaken us and we follow helplessly along. But is there a time when we should call a halt, when we should admit that we have made a terrible mistake? Why do you think the narrator could not do this?

At the end of the story it is clear that Jenny knew all about the boy's bragging lies. She had finished their relationship to help ease his pain and he had responded with cruel lies and deceptions. Why do you think Jenny said nothing? Why did she let the lies continue? What would you have done in the same situation?

Writing

The story ends with the narrator staring after Jenny as she goes down the corridor. Write a follow-up, telling what happened next. Did he go after her? Did he turn away and keep the memory? The choice is yours.

Write three or four pages from Jenny's diary, starting the day she finishes with the boy and covering the lies he soon starts to tell.

One of the most effective ways of setting mood is by using music. If you were turning Bearding the Dragon into a TV play which pieces of pop music would you use as background? Draw up a list and say why you have chosen them. (For example, when the boy sees Jenny coming down the road towards the tennis courts you could play Heartbeat; or, when he is lying on his bed in abject misery, you could play almost any song by Westlife.)

What would the boy's friends have said and done if he had admitted the truth? Write a page showing how they would have reacted to him.

Is there a time when you have told a lie, either to get out of trouble or to gain something you desperately wanted? Did it get you into even more trouble? Turn the incident into a story.

Reflection

▶ Bragging to improve your status is not nice but it is something that is often done. It is particularly unpleasant when it hurts somebody you care about. Ask pupils to reflect on whether or not they have ever done this.

▶ Most lies are easily seen through and while you may think you have got away with it, the chances are that you probably haven't. Often you end up telling more lies to cover the first – and that could really make you look stupid.

Session 9: Aunt Dotty and the Dog

Focus

▸ awkward relatives

▸ the pain that family brings

▸ revenge.

The story I am going to tell took place a long time ago. It happened one December when I was about eleven or twelve, maybe even thirteen. Time has a way of losing dates. But one thing I am sure about, it was the worst Christmas ever. Not because there was a shortage of presents. No, there were cartloads of them, all as necessary as ever. It was the worst Christmas simply because of Aunt Dotty and the dog.

The dog came first, two days before Christmas Eve. I was in the front room, lying happily in the warmth from the log fire and my unusual surroundings. The front room was the best room, used only for births, deaths and holidays like Easter Sunday or Christmas. So, now, to lie there with the heat from the fire searing my legs, a bowl of crisps at my left hand and the TV blasting out the weekly edition of Top of the Pops was the closest I had yet come to paradise. I should have known it was too good to last.

The door crashed suddenly open, hammering back against the old upright piano so that all its loose and jumbled keys sang out in a chorus of approaching doom. There was a panting like an express train and, when I looked up, the second cousin of the Hound of the Baskervilles was dribbling slime onto my face.

'Jesus Christ!' I yelled. 'Get it away from me.'

The dog was big, a crossbred Alsatian with a ferocious temper and yellow eyes that chilled you to the bone. What he was crossed with I did not know, a timber wolf I would have guessed! He was the pampered pet of my Uncle Jim, a vicious animal whose sudden approach we all feared like we feared vampires and the demons of our imagination.

'What's he doing here?' I wailed as the dog began to help himself from my bowl of crisps.

I tried to ease the container out of his reach but there was a menacing growl from the back of his throat and my courage quickly evaporated. I surrendered the crisps and in five seconds the bowl was empty.

My father, who seemed to be attached to the animal's collar by a length of string, hurled himself onto the settee and snorted.

'We've got him for Christmas,' he said. 'Uncle Jim's had a bit of a crisis. His mother has broken her hip so he's been called away. The whole family's gone with him. All except Fang. We've got to look after him until they come back after New Year.'

It was appalling. How could Jim's mother be so selfish as to break her hip just three days before Christmas? I frowned as Fang settled himself easily between the fire and me, his staring amber eyes defying me to question his right to the position of superiority.

'You'll have to take him for walks,' said my father. 'He's just dragged me up the road at fifty miles an hour. I'm bloody shattered.'

Thanks, Dad, I thought, that's really going to make my Christmas. I was right. Fang constantly demanded attention, his lead-weighted paws smashing into your groin whenever he wanted to be stroked or fed with dog biscuits. Five or six times a day I was dragged behind him, like a sweeping but powerless water-skier, as he drove for the nearby Common.

Once taken off the lead, however, Fang instantly disappeared, charging over the bracken covered slopes in a vain effort to fix his slavering jaws onto the wildlife of the area. Several times I tried slipping quietly home while he was out of sight but before I had gone fifty yards he would appear ahead of me on the path, barking loudly and demanding to be taken back to the Common. We must have spent hours up there.

Fang hated visitors. Three of my school friends called one morning and were dispatched, post haste, yelling in pain, the backsides missing from their trousers. Once he pinned the postman to the door step, waking the entire neighbourhood with his barking and spreading the contents of the mail bag across the street. Like the remnants of a paper chase the Christmas cards lay, accusing and angry, in the road.

The worst thing he did, however, was on Christmas morning. The turkey was taken out of the oven and left to stand, golden and magnificent, on the kitchen table. Its succulent aroma filled the room.

'Don't touch it,' my mother warned. 'It's hot.'

Of course, the inevitable happened. A few minutes later my mother's piercing shriek alerted us to trouble and we hurtled like a pack of rampant firemen for the kitchen door. The table was empty but lying full length on the floor was Fang. The last turkey leg was just disappearing down his gullet.

'I'll kill him!' screamed my mother, advancing towards the animal with the carving knife.

Fang had nothing if not a good sense of self-preservation. He knew when to beat a hasty retreat. The fact that he bowled over the entire family in his effort to escape was a mere trifle that did not even begin to enter his dinosaur brain.

I think, possibly, we could have put up with Fang, loutish and unpleasant as he was, if the situation had not been made so much worse by the arrival of Aunt Dotty. It was in that strange, empty lull between Christmas and New Year's Eve and her arrival was like a hurricane.

Short and tiny, as frail as a china figurine, Aunt Dotty's appearance totally belied her power. Like Genghis Khan or Attila the Hun, her visits always left you breathless and gasping for relief. Angry, self-opinionated, selfish – every unpleasant adjective I could think of could be applied to her. Luckily she lived out in the country and so her visits were rare and of short duration. It was scant consolation.

My father greeted me with the news of her arrival when I returned from one of my morning walks with Fang.

'Thanks,' I said. 'That really makes Christmas complete.'

Dad was thoughtful, a thin frown masking his face.

'Listen, you know what she's like, as nosey as Old Nick. Whatever you do, don't tell her that I've just redecorated upstairs. She'll be up there quicker than you can blink, snooping around, finding fault with everything. At her age the effort will probably kill her.'

I made no reply but grinned, wickedly, to myself.

'Oh, one other thing,' added Dad, 'she hates dogs. Make sure Fang is out of the way while she's here.'

Aunt Dotty sortied into the house half an hour later, a whirlwind of orders, demands and disruption. Hurriedly, I dragged Fang out of the hallway, Dotty's voice screeching in my ears.

'Get that awful animal out of my sight!'

I tried pushing him out through the back door but he refused to leave the warm house. I tried tying his lead to the kitchen table but the moment I left the room both dog and table bounded through the door after me. Eventually, in desperation, I took him upstairs. Fang had always fancied my parents' bedroom and loved nothing more than to lie elegantly across their bed. My mother had forbidden him to go anywhere near the place, an order he seemed to understand but also to resent with every ounce of his self-centred soul.

So, now, to be allowed to indulge himself, to sprawl across their new bedspread – Fang was in ecstasy. I closed the door and crept downstairs to rejoin Aunt Dotty and my parents.

It was not the easiest of afternoons. Aunt Dotty soon had me running around the house, fetching her a glass of sherry, a piece of Christmas cake – even my latest school report. Anything to keep me on the move and at her bidding.

'I'm really not as young as I was,' she said. 'I find moving about a little difficult.'

You just wait, I told myself, we'll soon see how mobile you are, you arrogant old harridan. Just wait. At last, however, the conversation turned to work around the house.

'And do you help your mother, boy?' she demanded. 'Do you assist your father with his decorating or in the garden? Well, do you, boy?'

She used the word 'boy' like an accusation. She knew my name of course but she had never addressed me as anything except 'boy.' Now I glanced at her and grinned.

'Of course,' I responded smugly. 'I always do my fair share. I even helped Dad wallpaper the bedroom last…'

I stopped, glancing quickly across at my father. He glared at me. Dotty sat up and stared at my father.

'So you've just redecorated, have you?' she said, her fertile interest caught by my words. 'Your bedroom, is it?'

Dad nodded, glumly.

'Yes, Dot, our bedroom, bathroom, landings, the lot. New furniture as well.'

Aunt Dotty's eyes gleamed, her curiosity alive and breathing, deadly as a snake that has been suddenly disturbed.

'I wonder,' she said, 'perhaps I could…'

'Have some more tea, Dotty,' said my mother and we moved quickly on to other topics.

Yet Aunt Dotty was not to be denied. Twenty minutes later she decided that she needed to visit the bathroom.

'Would you like one of us to help you up the stairs?' asked my father.

Dotty fixed him with a glare, her back arched and disdain oozing out of every pore.

'I am very far from helpless, I'll have you know.'

'But I thought you said you found moving about difficult?' I reminded her.

Dotty shook her head. She didn't even bother to look at me.

'I am quite capable of climbing a few stairs, boy.'

We lapsed into sullen silence as she ambled out of the door. Dad glared at me but said nothing. We waited for Dotty's return – and kept on waiting. Five minutes passed, then ten. There was no sign of her.

'Perhaps she's dead?' I said, hopefully.

My mother sighed and shook her head in despair.

'You'd better go and look for her,' she told my father. 'Mind you, you won't have to look far. We all know what she'll be doing.'

Despite myself I could not help grinning. What Dotty would be doing was snooping around Mum and Dad's newly decorated bedroom. And in that bedroom was…

At that moment somebody dropped an atom bomb on the top floor of our house. There was a bang, which shook and rattled every brick and window frame in the building. Rising like a banshee wail, a shriek of terror sliced through the air. It was accompanied by an insistent and regular thumping, exactly as if somebody was drumming their heels on the floor above our heads. And over it all came a deep-throated roar, a growl of vengeance and anger that quickly confirmed my suspicions.

'What the hell is that?' said my father.

We took the stairs three at a time, charging onto the upstairs landing like a trio of rugby forwards. The door to my parent's bedroom was wide open and there, stretched out on the floor, with Fang standing astride her prostrate body, was Aunt Dotty.

She was rigid with fear, eyes wide and staring. Fang's foam-flecked jaws were just three inches from her face and he kept up a low-pitched growl that sent a shiver of terror up my backbone. His breath had misted Aunt Dotty's glasses and perhaps that was just as well as she was unable to see more than just a vague outline of the creature that had pinned her to the floor.

Straining every muscle, my father and I dragged Fang away. He came unwillingly, growling and snapping out at us in temper. Mum helped Aunt Dotty to her feet and led her gently down to the front room.

'A demon,' I heard her wail as she clutched desperately at the banister rail. 'It's the devil come to haunt me.'

My father glanced at me, unable to prevent the faint beginnings of a smile from cracking the edges of his mouth. Dotty did not stay long. Unsteady, complaining bitterly about her treatment, she was helped to her car and drove away, vowing never to visit us again

'Twenty-five years it's taken to stop that old biddy nosing around my house,' said my mother, 'twenty-five years! That'll teach her not to go snooping.'

She smiled at Fang who had now taken up his usual position in front of the fire.

'There's a good dog,' she said.

Fang gulped. Eyes twinkling, Mum went off to the kitchen and came back with a large ham bone for the dog. He took it cautiously, waiting for the sting in the tail. When Mum patted him kindly on the head, a sudden and confused look of defeat spread across his features. Like a playful kitten he rolled over onto his back as my mother began to gently tickle his belly.

Christmas may not have been up to much but it looked like it was going to be a good New Year.

Activities and Discussion

The narrator is devastated at having his Christmas spoiled by the arrival of Fang. Is he being selfish or realistic? How would you have felt in the same circumstances?

Does Aunt Dotty deserve understanding or is she just an awful old woman who gets what she deserves? Old people are often demanding but does this mean that they are not worthy of respect and courtesy? Does Aunt Dotty receive either of these in this story?

When there is extra work to be done, like walking the dog in this story, it is always the youngest member of the family who gets the chore. Is this fair? Should the job not be shared out more evenly?

When the narrator locks Fang in the bedroom do you think he does it deliberately, knowing that Aunt Dotty will go snooping and find herself faced by the dog? Or is it a total accident?

Members of your family often put all sorts of strains on you when they come to visit. Just because they are relatives it doesn't mean you actually have to like them. Aunt Dotty certainly falls into this category. Do people have to earn respect and your affection or, in the case of family members, do they deserve it automatically?

Think about respect. What is it? Do we respect others? Do they respect us? How can we show respect to other human beings?

Writing

What would have happened if Fang had been even more vicious? Might he have savaged or even killed Aunt Dotty? What would the boy have done then? Imagine that things have gone further than he ever intended. Tell the story of what happened next.

Turn the story into a short play for voices. There need be no stage directions and there should be a narrator – not necessarily the boy – who fills in details that cannot be given in the dialogue.

Who is your worst relative or, maybe, your worst friend? Do you know someone who embarrasses you every time they open their mouth? Tell the story of the most awful things they have ever done. Remember how they made you feel with their actions. You can make your story funny or tragic.

Everybody loves animal stories. In the library find as many novels or stories about animals as you possibly can. Which ones are your favourite and why?

Christmas can be a hugely enjoyable time, full of fun and laughter. It can also be lonely and depressing. How do you feel about Christmas? Why do you like or dislike it? Write one page, giving your views. Give the reasons why you have made your choice.

Reflection

- Sometimes we do things and get the wrong reaction. We need to consider what we should do in situations like that. Should we change our approach, should we apologise? What should we do?

- Always consider the possible consequences of your actions. Your motives may be good but how are they interpreted? Making appropriate choices is partly about facing up to the consequences of those choices.

Session 10: Choices

Focus

▶ drug taking

▶ loneliness and vulnerability

▶ being accepted

▶ shielding others from retribution.

Dionne gazed up at the soaring arches of the Eiffel Tower and felt incredibly lonely and afraid. How much longer, she asked herself, before I can go home?

When the idea of a school trip to France had first been announced it had seemed like a great opportunity. The chance of ten days away from home, seeing and visiting all the places Dionne had only ever dreamed about before now, was far too good to be missed.

'It'll be such fun,' Helen had said, excitedly. 'Imagine it, wandering down the boulevards, taking coffee in all those pavement cafes. We'll be like two elegant French ladies.'

Then she had paused and looked at Dionne from beneath dark eyebrows.

'Think your mum will let you go?'

It had not been easy. Dionne's mother had always thought that Helen was a bad influence on her daughter. And, of course, money was tight. Her brother Leroy was just about to start school and that, on its own, was a very expensive business.

'Oh, please, Mum?' Dionne had cajoled. 'I'll get a Saturday job and I'll work to pay towards it. Please Mum?'

And eventually her mother had agreed. She would find the money somehow.

'Although the thought of you two on the loose in Paris,' she said, shaking her head, 'doesn't fill me with a lot of confidence.'

As the day of departure drew closer Dionne felt the excitement growing huge and echoing in her belly. She just knew that she and Helen were going to have a great time.

And then came disaster. Two days before the trip Helen fell from the wall bars in the school gym and broke her leg. There was no way she would be able to make the school holiday.

'I'm so sorry, Dionne,' she cried from her hospital bed. 'But you'll still have a great time. Remember to send me a postcard.'

Dionne shook her head. 'I don't think I want to go without you. It won't be the same.'

There had been a furious row when she mentioned it to her mother. Anger filled the room, anger so thick you could almost touch it.

'Not go? What you talking about, girl? You think I'm made of money?'

She had swept out of the room, tension and hurt swirling around her head. Dionne heard her mumbling to herself as she slammed around the tiny kitchen.

'I've scrimped and saved so you can go on this trip, girl. And believe me, you'll be going, even if I have to carry you there myself.'

So she had gone and been lonely ever since. She knew none of the others on the trip. They were all older or had their own groups of friends. None of them talked to her and the pain of feeling so different, of being left out, was real and livid inside her. Without Helen, hers was the only black face in the party. She didn't know if that was a consideration with the others but it certainly added to the feeling of being alone and apart.

'Only another five days,' she whispered to herself as she stood, now, beneath the Eiffel Tower. 'Then I can go home in peace.'

'Been up it yet?'

She spun around at the sound of the voice. Flustered, suddenly embarrassed, she found herself staring into the face of Tom Bowen. He was tall and handsome, one of the sixth form boys everyone in her year so admired.

'Sorry?'

He gestured upwards with his thumb. Dionne shook her head.

'Come on, then, let's go.'

And that was how it had begun. Tom stuck close to her for the rest of the day, happily pointing out the landmarks and places of interest along the river. He knew Paris well, having visited the city with his parents on many occasions, and was more than content to share his knowledge.

During the long afternoon they strolled together along the Left Bank, deep in conversation, and stopped to buy coffee and cake from one of the many street vendors who were hawking their wares. It felt so good, standing and walking beside Tom, so natural and easy. She felt grown-up and independent.

As evening fell over the city and its bridges they ambled back to their hotel. Suddenly Dionne felt Tom reach out for her hand. Their fingers entwined and for the first time in days she was idyllically happy.

When Tom knocked on her door a few hours later Dionne noticed immediately that there was something different about the boy. Gone was the easy affability and now he was almost buzzing with tension. He stood before her, high and excited.

'Come on, Dionne,' he hissed. 'Let's go and find some life in this dead-end city.'

His eyes sparkled and he was almost hopping from foot to foot in his eagerness to be away. Dionne stared at him but said nothing.

'Are you coming?' he asked, moving quickly away down the corridor.

'We're not supposed to leave the hotel,' Dionne protested. 'Miss Wicks said…'

'Bugger what Miss Wicks said!'

Tom turned and came back to her door. Casually, he smiled at her. It did not hide the raw energy that was obviously churning inside him.

'Look, kid, I'm going out. There's a club close by, just around the corner. I saw it when we walked back earlier tonight. Live music, cheap drinks – just what I need after a day parading around this damned city.'

He paused and, with real effort, managed to contain his excitement.

'Dionne, I'm out of here. You can come or you can stay. After all there must be something good on telly – in French, of course. The choice is yours.'

Put like that there really wasn't any choice to be made. Dionne knew she should stay in her room, knew that by going with Tom she would be confirming all her mother's worst fears. But he had asked her to go with him and there was no way she was going to refuse.

'Give me two minutes,' she said.

The club was dark and noisy. Music pulsed and rolled out through the narrow doorway, cloaking the steady stream of people who constantly wandered in and out of the place. For a brief moment Dionne wondered if she would actually be allowed in, after all she seemed so much younger than most of the men and women. But the doorman did not even give her a second glance. Soon, they were seated in a dark alcove inside the club, not far away from the tiny stage.

'Great, isn't it?' shouted Tom.

Dionne sipped at her wine, wincing at the taste and trying to hide her reaction from Tom. She had never liked the taste of alcohol. Even the communion wine in church back home made her gag and turned her stomach sick. But Tom had bought the drink for her and she thought it would be churlish to refuse.

As the evening wore on Tom seemed to be slowly calming down. It had been quite strange. During the day he had been so attentive, so polite. But tonight he had seemed hyperactive, manic almost. Dionne was glad to see him getting back to his normal self. It did not last long.

'Got to go to the toilet,' Tom suddenly announced.

He lurched to his feet and strode away. When he came back he was alive and electric once again. His feet tapped in time to the music and he had great difficulty in keeping still.

'Are you alright?' Dionne asked.

Tom grinned. 'Never better,' he said.

Dionne stared around the club. It was full of young people, dancing or simply standing around and talking. Everyone seemed so much older than her. Instinctively, she knew that she did not like the place but, as long as they were there, she wished that Tom would ask her to dance. He did not.

For over an hour they sat there, talking and drinking – or, rather, Tom talked and drank while she sipped quietly at her original glass of wine.

'I think we should be getting back,' Dionne said, at last, 'before somebody finds out we've gone.'

Tom smiled at her, blissfully unconcerned, and shrugged.

'Who cares? They can't really expect us to stay in that stupid bloody hotel all night. Not when we've got all this out here, just waiting for us.'

He glanced around, almost furtively. Slowly he reached into his trouser pocket.

'You're too uptight, Dionne. Maybe this will help.'

He held out a small twist of silver paper. Dionne stared at it, then up into Tom's eager face.

'What is it?' she asked.

Tom glanced around again, as if making sure that nobody was watching. He need not have bothered. Everyone else in the club was engrossed in their own business. To them Tom and Dionne did not even exist.

'Never mind what it is. Try it.'

Carefully, he unrolled the foil. Inside lay a small stash of white powder. Dionne felt her stomach turn over.

'Drugs?' she said.

Tom closed his fist over the packet. 'Hush. Don't broadcast it. Just take it.'

Dionne shook her head. She had never been interested in drugs. It frightened her, the drug scene, scared her half to death. It was dangerous and illegal, that much she knew. And apart from anything else her mother would kill her if she ever took any.

'I don't want to,' she said.

Tom snarled. His face twisted into an ugly sneer that Dionne had never seen before.

'Listen up, girl,' he said, reaching over to grab her arm. 'We're going to have a good time tonight. And we can't do that if you're so bloody uptight you're liable to break in half.'

He paused. 'You do want to be with me, don't you? Because if you don't, there's plenty more back in the hotel who do.'

Dionne's mind was racing. Of course she wanted to be with him. Who wouldn't? Tom made her feel so mature, so grown-up. She certainly did not want to be alone and lonely again. She had been so pleased when he had picked her out. She didn't know why and she didn't really care. He had chosen her and that was that. She was so grateful.

'Well?'

Tom was glaring at her now. What would her mother say if she took the packet? But then, her mother need never know. It wouldn't hurt, would it, just this once, to make Tom happy? No, it wouldn't hurt.

She reached out and gingerly took the silver foil from Tom's hand. He grinned at her and winked.

*   *   *   *   *

Bright pinpoints of sharp light suddenly stabbed into Dionne's brain. They hurt like needles being jabbed into her head. Slowly, warily, she opened her eyes.

'She's awake,' said a voice.

The light was coming from a set of arc lamps in the ceiling. Four figures were clustered around her bed. Bed? Where was she? As if guessing her thoughts the voice spoke again.

'You're in hospital, Dionne.'

It was Miss Wicks. The other people she did not recognise but they wore white coats and one of them had a stethoscope around his neck.

'Hospital?' she croaked.

Her head ached and when she tried to move her arms they felt as if they were made of lead.

'What happened?'

Miss Wicks leaned over and took her hand.

'That's what we want you to tell us, Dionne.'

She paused and glanced, briefly, at one of the men. He nodded.

'You took something, Dionne. When they found you outside the club you were unconscious. You'd been sick – you nearly choked on your own vomit. Luckily you had our hotel address in your jeans pocket. It was a good job we decided to make you all carry it.'

Dionne nodded, gratefully. But the movement made her head swim. She closed her eyes and tried to think back. She could remember nothing after Tom had given her the silver foil packet. Tom! He had given her the…

Her eyes jerked open once again.

'Tom,' she said, urgently. 'Where's Tom?'

Miss Wicks was clearly puzzled. 'Tom? Tom Bowen? He's back at the hotel. Why, Dionne?'

Dionne said nothing. After a few moments the man with the stethoscope, a doctor she supposed, asked if she would like to sit up.

'Please,' she whispered.

Sitting in the hospital bed felt a lot better than lying down. At least the world stayed still when she was in this position.

'So,' said Miss Wicks, eventually, 'what happened?'

Dionne shrugged her shoulders. 'I went to the club, after everyone had gone to bed.'

'But why, Dionne? You knew that was against the rules for the trip.'

She stared at Dionne through suddenly narrowed eyes. 'Did you go on your own?

Dionne lowered her head. Miss Wicks indicated the two men who, so far, had not spoken a single word.

'These men are police. They know you took something, some illegal substance, at the club. They want to know what it was and they want to know who gave it to you. They are the police, Dionne, French drug squad. This is a very serious situation, girl. You almost died last night. You need to cooperate fully.'

Dionne felt tears gathering at the corners of her eyes. Fear, huge and solid as a fist, had gathered in her windpipe. What have I done, she asked herself? What will Mum say? Damn that Tom, it was his fault; he gave me the filthy stuff.

She looked up and saw four pairs of eyes fixed on her face. She had to tell them the truth.

At that moment, beyond the glass viewing panel in the door, she saw Tom. His face was close up to the glass and was pale and frightened. She thought that she could smell his fear. He was staring in through the glass at the people who were gathered around her bed and, as she stared at him, Tom caught her gaze. His smile was strained and afraid. What is he doing here, Dionne asked herself silently, why has he come?

It was a question she did not need to answer. He was here because he was afraid. He was here to make sure she did not tell everyone where she had got the drugs.

'Well?' said Miss Wicks.

Tom, her mother, Miss Wicks, everything and everyone – the images went hurtling around her brain. What should she do, what should she say?

'Help me,' she mumbled to herself.

'We're trying to, dear,' said Miss Wicks. 'But we need to know where you got the drugs. Otherwise you take the blame and they get away, scot-free.'

Dionne swallowed hard and stared at the teacher's kind green eyes. It was time to make the final choice.

Activities and Discussion

When Helen fell and injured herself should Dionne have dropped out of the trip, knowing that she would now have no friends going with her? Was her mother right to insist that she went on the trip? What was the motivation for insisting that Dionne went?

How do you think Dionne felt when Tom suddenly noticed her? She had been lonely and vulnerable for too long and, now, to come to the notice of an older, handsome boy like Tom was just too much. When he asked her to go out, breaking the rules of the trip, what should she have done? To refuse would have meant losing his friendship, to accept meant breaking the rules. Dionne was in a dilemma. Did she make the right choice?

Tom offered Dionne drugs and when she refused he used emotional blackmail to try and persuade her. What should she have done at that point? She would have needed to be a very strong character indeed to refuse and leave the club. Was Dionne strong enough to do that? Was she right to think that her mother need never know? Or was this just a fantasy?

At the end of the story Dionne is faced by yet another dilemma. Should she shield Tom from retribution? To do so would mean taking the blame herself. Yet he was the one who gave her the drugs in the first place. What should she do?

Did Tom care about Dionne or was he simply using her for his own ends?

Where do you stand on drug abuse? Discuss the issue of soft and hard drugs, legalising cannabis and so on.

Writing

Write two endings to the story, one where Dionne tells the police who gave her the drugs, one where she takes the blame herself. Produce a page of writing on each of them.

Imagine that Helen did not injure herself; imagine that she made the trip. How might things have been different? Write the last two pages of Dionne's diary of the trip, telling how things have gone, all the things they have done and the places they have seen.

In the library find out all you can about drugs. Identify four commonly used substances, their effects and dangers. Write a paragraph about each of them.

Write a story about a boy or girl who becomes hooked on drugs. Start with their first experience, perhaps with soft drugs; finish with the inevitable decline and possible death that comes with addiction to substances like heroin.

Retell the story, this time using Tom as the narrator. Writing in first person, try to show how Tom felt and what he intended to achieve by giving Dionne the drugs in the nightclub.

Reflection

▸ Somebody who is lonely and vulnerable, like Dionne in the story, is easy prey to the people who peddle drugs. Do drug addicts deserve our scorn or sympathy?

Ask the pupils to consider this question very carefully. It is for them to reflect upon, we do not need an answer. However, the question may well elicit some response and debate, depending upon the experiences of the young people.

Session 11: To Be a Star

> **Focus**
> ▸ the search for fame
> ▸ fame – rather than success
> ▸ using others.

Tina felt the excitement tingling like sunburn in her belly. This was it, her big chance. She nervously straightened the collar of her dress, stared at Mark and tried to smile. The boy shrugged, nonchalantly, and turned away.

How could he be so cool about it, Tina wondered? Didn't he know that the next three minutes could bring them more fame and fortune than they had ever dreamed about? Didn't he know that this was a chance in a million?

All her life, as long as she could remember, Tina had wanted to be famous. It didn't matter what she was famous for, as long as people noticed her whenever she walked down the road, as long as they pointed her out and whispered, 'There goes Tina.' Above all she longed for the day when thousands of worshipping fans would stand in a line to ask for her autograph.

'And they will,' she whispered. 'After tonight.'

She had begun singing lessons early, when she was five or six. After all, every time she turned on the television there was some new singing sensation being hailed by managers and programme presenters as the latest and most incredible star yet to appear in the entertainment industry. Singing and dancing certainly seemed the best bet for fame and fortune. And so that was the way she went. They had been her life ever since, all through primary school and her early teenage years. They were all she lived for, knowing that one day they would propel her to the top of the tree.

'I'm going to be famous, Mum,' she constantly told her mother. 'More famous than Britney Spears. Or Madonna.'

Her mother nodded approvingly. She was behind Tina all the way. New clothes, new shoes, acting lessons – whatever it took, her mother would provide it. Not everyone felt quite the same about her ambitions, however.

'Concentrate on your studies a bit more,' her teachers told her. 'You need qualifications to get on in this world. You'll never make a living out of music.'

Even her friends soon became fed up with her constant seeking for fame and glory.

'You're obsessed with being famous,' they told her. 'It's getting to be boring, Tina, real boring. Let's talk about something else.'

Friends might come and friends might go, Tina decided, but her dream lived on. Nothing would ever replace that.

When she saw the notice on the Leisure Centre board Tina stopped and stared. She felt as if she had been hit by a thunderbolt. Her heart pounded in her chest and she knew that this was it. Her great moment had come.

'Auditions!' the poster declared. 'Wanted – singers for a new TV show. Pop Duos, this is your chance to appear on TV on the new 'Hall of Fame' Talent Show.'

Eagerly, Tina jotted down the details and raced home to tell her mother. Already her mind was running wild. She would win the audition, appear on the TV show and the rest would be history. Fame and fortune would follow as surely as New Year followed Christmas Day.

It was only later, sitting and trying to calm her racing nerves, that Tina suddenly realised there was a problem. She gave a start and sat bolt upright in the chair.

'What is it?' asked her mother.

'The contest, Mum, the audition. I've just realised. It's for a duo.'

Her mother stared, hardly understanding. Tina shook her head in exasperation. Sometimes her mother could be so thick!

'A duo? Two people? This contest, it's for two people singing together. A duo, Mum, a bloody duo.'

Sitting there, now, Tina remembered reading something about it in one of the music papers she bought every week. Duos, the article said, were to be the coming thing in pop music. Tina leapt to her feet and rummaged around in the stack of magazines at the side of the settee. Finding what she wanted Tina threw herself back into the chair and turned to the second page of the paper.

'Forget groups or solo singers,' the article read, 'duos are back in fashion. Remember Simon and Garfunkel? Sonny and Cher? Well, now they're back. Two voices are definitely better than one.'

At the time Tina had doubted it. But, now, here was proof positive. Even the TV talent programmes, the reality shows that were so popular these days, were going that way. Duos were obviously the future of pop music.

'So what are you going to do?' asked her mother.

Tina shrugged.

'I'll just have to find myself a partner, somebody to sing with me.'

She turned towards her mother.

'You know how much this means to me. There's no way I'm going to miss this chance of being on TV. I really do want to be famous, Mum, so famous that everybody in the country will know my name.'

Her mother smiled at her.

'The country? What's wrong with the world?'

Tina found her singing partner far sooner than she had ever imagined possible. In school the very next day she passed the music room on her way to choir practice. From inside the room came the crystal-clear tones of a boy's voice. It was melodic and superbly pitched. It was perfect.

Peering in through the door Tina saw Mark standing in front of the piano. She knew him, of course, had seen him in classes or at choir practice, but she had never realised what a beautiful voice he had.

'You sound like Ronan Keating,' she announced. 'Only twice as good.'

Mark started and turned to face her, the music and melody cut off mid-phrase.

'Don't stop,' Tina said, advancing into the room. 'Let me hear it to the end.'

The boy turned back to the piano and continued with his song. He played and sang without a trace of embarrassment. And it was so beautiful that Tina could have wept. However, convincing Mark that they should sing together was not easy.

'I don't want to sing for a career,' he said. 'I've got plans for my future. I want to go to university.'

'I don't want to sing, either,' Tina continued. 'I just want to be famous.'

It had taken her time – so much time that she missed her choir practice, something she had never done before – but, at last, she managed to get him to agree.

'You really won't regret it, Mark,' she said. 'Once we win the competition you can do whatever you like, you can carry on or pack it all in as far as I'm concerned. Appearing on the TV show is the key. Once you get noticed, anything's possible. And anyway, the money is bound to be useful when you go to university.'

Mark nodded. He really didn't mind, one way or the other.

'Well, it's worth a shot, I suppose – if it helps you.'

After that Tina's mind became focused on the audition. She spent hours preparing her outfit for the show, experimenting with her hair and working out her moves, even down to the way she would walk out onto the stage. Appearance was everything. She needed to make sure that she looked good on the big night.

'What about practising our number?' asked Mark one evening after school.

They had decided to perform an Andrew Lloyd Webber song, No Matter What. It came from a musical, Whistle Down the Wind, and suited their voices perfectly. It would be sure to bring the house down, Tina had gloated. Mark agreed – as long as they could practise and perfect their close harmonies.

Now, however, Tina simply shook her head.

'Sorry, no can do. I've got a fitting for my dress.'

Mark frowned at her.

'Tina,' he said, 'if we don't get the song right, it won't matter what you look like. It's a song contest, not a fashion show.'

He sighed and moved away.

'It's up to you,' he said. 'You're the one who's so desperate to win.'

She had managed to find time to rehearse, eventually. And Tina knew that they sounded good. Mark's voice was so pure, reaching like crystal filaments into the air. It blended with her own richer tones in a perfect mix that enchanted everyone in school who came to hear them.

'You're bound to win,' Tina's friends told her. 'You'll be rich and famous soon.'

So now, here they were, waiting backstage for their turn. Tina had listened, admittedly only with half an ear – she was really only interested in her own performance – to the other singers. As far as she was concerned there was only one other pairing that came anywhere close to her and Mark, and Mark had noticed them too.

'See that couple over there? Tony and Debbie, I think they're called.'

He indicated towards a pretty blonde girl and her partner who were standing and watching the acts from the wings. Even as they stared at them, the girl turned, noticed their interest and smiled. Mark smiled back and raised his thumb.

'They're pretty good. They just gave the best performance I've seen tonight.'

Tina snorted.

'Yes, well, we haven't sung yet, have we? Yeah, they're not bad but they aren't in our league. OK, she's got a fair enough voice but he's pretty crap. And anyway, her dress isn't a patch on mine.'

When their turn came to sing Tina knew they performed really well. Maybe she did hit one or two flat notes but nobody really noticed. For a moment Tina wished she had had the sense to rehearse a bit more but it was only a fleeting thought. What the hell, she looked great and she moved great. What more did they want? And anyway, Mark's voice was superb. It would get them through.

The audience, lots of them friends from school, stamped and cheered and Tina wallowed in the applause. She never wanted to leave the stage and would have happily stood there in the footlights forever.

When the judges came backstage to give their verdict, Tina could hardly contain her excitement. This was it, fame and fortune lay just ahead.

'I won't keep you long,' said the head judge. 'Show business is a cut-throat affair and if any of you are interested in making it a career you'll have to get used to hard reviews. I won't insult you by pretending you were all good. Let's be honest, some of the acts we saw tonight were pretty poor.'

He paused and stared at the eager faces.

'We want just one pair from this audition. That's what we have been looking for, one pair from each audition we hold.'

This is it, thought Tina, they want Mark and me. I've done it. I'm going to be on TV, I'm going to be famous.

'Unfortunately,' continued the judge, 'no single pair really impressed us tonight. So what we are going to do is take singers from two different pairs, put them together and make one duo that's worthy of appearing on the 'Hall of Fame' show.'

'Me, me, me,' hissed Tina, 'make it me.'

'Mark and Debbie, we'd like you to sing together. We'd like you to go forward to Hall of Fame.'

It took three or four seconds for the words to sink into Tina's brain. She hadn't been chosen. They'd taken Mark and that stupid bloody Debbie. They couldn't do that, they couldn't split up the pairings. It was her right to be chosen. Who was this damned Debbie? Nobody knew her, she was just a simpering little brat! All right, maybe she could sing but she couldn't move. And her dress sense was awful.

Before she realised it, Tina found herself shouting.

'You can't do this.'

The judge glared at her, his eyes cold and disinterested.

'We can do whatever we want, love. This audition tonight was all about finding the right people for the TV show. And we think we've done exactly that.'

'But it's not fair!'

Sighing, the judge quickly crossed the room and took Tina by the arm.

'Fair doesn't come into it. Mark and Debbie have the best voices, that was clear to everybody.'

'But she looks awful. And she can't dance.'

The judge shook his head

'We can work on things like that. If you haven't got the basic talent, kid, you can put all the gloss you like on top. It won't work. Mark and Debbie have got the basics. I reckon when we put them together they'll make us a fortune.'

Tina felt her head swimming. She felt sick and knew that beads of sweat had broken out across her forehead.

'But what about me?' she said. 'This was my big chance. I was going to be famous. What happens to me now?'

The judge shrugged.

'Go back to school and get yourself a career. You're good, love, but you're not that good. Not good enough to make it at the top level. I'm not even that sure about Debbie. But, Mark? Well, that voice is solid gold.'

Tina felt her world collapsing around her. Her legs trembled and she felt faint. The judge moved away, then stopped and glanced back over his shoulder.

'A word of advice. A little less concentration on fame, a bit more on talent and performance. That's if you really do want to get on in this business.'

He moved away, shepherding Mark and Debbie towards the door.

'Mark,' Tina called. 'Don't do it, Mark.'

The boy stared at her, hesitating at the doorway. Still unsure, he shrugged. And at that moment something exploded inside Tina.

'You bastard!' she shouted. 'This was meant to be my night. Hell, you didn't even want to enter, you selfish, scheming bastard!'

The judge leaned forward and whispered into Mark's ear. Without looking back they went out of the room.

Tina slumped against the edge of a low divan. It was over, the dream was over. As she saw her mother striding expectantly across the room towards her she felt tears pricking against her eyelids and knew that the future was bleak – bleak and empty.

Activities and Discussion

Tina is desperate to be famous. Everything in her life is geared towards achieving this end. It is the trappings of fame that attract her, not the desire to succeed at singing. Indeed, singing and dancing are just the vehicles to enable her to be famous. What do you think about this? Is it the right attitude? Should you try to achieve fame or should you try to succeed, at whatever it is you do? Is there any difference between the two things?

Reality TV shows offer instant fame to the participants. Shows like Big Brother and Fame Academy propel people into the limelight. What happens if they are not emotionally ready for such exposure? What happens to those, like Tina in the story, who fail? Do they need someone there to support them or pick them up afterwards? And what happens to them if there is no one?

What does Tina's future hold for her once she fails at the audition? Do you think she will try again? Will she take the judge's advice? Will she give it all up and concentrate on passing her exams?

Tina unashamedly uses Mark to help her achieve what she wants. Yet it backfires on her. Was she right to use another person in this way? It could be said that, in the end, Mark actually uses Tina. Certainly the TV company uses everybody. How do you feel about people using other people? Have you ever used somebody in order to get what you wanted?

Tina has abandoned everything to search for fame. Is this the right thing to do? Should you always have other options so that if you fail in one thing you can easily turn to another? Or should you set out your goals, your targets, and then go for them with every piece of energy you possess?

Fame is one thing; success in your chosen field is something different. Why do people seem to choose fame? What is it that makes people want to be recognised, rather than work hard at a particular job?

Writing

If Tina won the contest, if she succeeded in her ambition, then her life would change. Imagine this has happened. Invent a Fact File for Tina, showing her successes after the contest. (For example, May 2005 – wins audition; July 2005 – wins the Hall of Fame contest; Sept 2005 – first record released, with Mark; Oct 2005 – splits with Mark and becomes a solo singer.)

What happens after Tina fails the audition? Write an account of her trip home with her mother, her tears and her upset. Include her decision about what she intends to do next.

Rewrite the story from Mark's point of view. You need to consider his feelings. Did he really want to take part in the contest? What did he feel like when he was chosen and Tina was not?

What are your feelings about 'Reality TV'? Do you think it is a good thing or just a way of providing cheap entertainment? Do people go on to make careers for themselves after appearing on one of these shows or do they quickly disappear from the public gaze? Write down your feelings, giving points in favour and points against. At the end, however, you need to make a judgement.

Find out about 'one hit wonders': people who had moments of success and then faded from view. You should visit your library for information – The Guinness Book of Hit Singles is a good place to start. Write a couple of pages about these people: their careers, their lives and what they are doing now.

Reflection

▶ Fame or achievement, which is the most important? Ask yourself if you can have both. Where should you be putting your effort?

▶ If you had the opportunity to appear on one of the 'Reality TV' shows, what would you do? What do you want to do with your life, what is it that you want to achieve? If you could have anything you desired, would you opt for fame and fortune? Or would you be more concerned about achieving something special in your career?

Session 12: Baby Won't you Drive my Car?

 Focus

▸ criminal behaviour

▸ antisocial behaviour

▸ acceptance by the group

▸ actions and consequences.

'What on earth is going on over there?'

Mitch pointed towards a large group of boys who were huddled together at the far side of the yard. Loud laughter, aggressive and arrogant, echoed across the playground, surrounding the group and giving them a sense of power. Peter followed Mitch's outstretched arm and sneered.

'Oh, that's only Deano and his mates. They're probably just bragging about last night's car.'

'Car? What do you mean, car?'

Mitch was curious. He knew Deano, of course. Everybody in town knew Deano. Mitch even took one or two lessons in the same set as him and they nodded to one another across the street sometimes. But that was about the full extent of their contact.

'Stealing cars, driving them around,' said Peter, 'that's what they're into. TDA it's called. Or TWOC.'

Mitch stared at him, not understanding.

'TDA,' said Peter, 'stands for taking and driving away. TWOC is taking without owners consent.'

'You seem to know a lot about it,' said Mitch.

Peter shrugged.

'When your dad's a policeman you tend to pick up all the jargon.'

He wandered away towards the main classroom block. Mitch stared at Deano and his group. They were loud and boisterous and a curious air of danger seemed to surround them. And yet there was an attraction as well. Mitch felt himself drawn towards the group, towards the tall and dominating figure of Deano. Almost without realising it he started to inch towards the group.

He was ten yards short when one of Deano's friends looked up and saw him. Casually he nudged Deano in the side.

'Company.'

Everyone turned towards him. Mitch felt the colour rush to his face and he moved quickly away.

'Hey, Mitch.'

He recognised Deano's nasal tones and paused. Glancing back over his shoulder, he saw the boy's cropped head jerking, beckoning him into the group.

'Come and join us. Listen to this.'

A sudden warmth coursed through his chest. He hadn't realised quite how much he craved this acceptance. There was companionship here, rough and ready, maybe, but companionship nonetheless. So he stood alongside Deano and listened to the tale of bravado.

'A hundred and twenty we was doing, down that road behind the Leisure Centre. The bloody car was sliding all over the place. And then, what did we see but a bloody police car at the bottom of the street. Blocking the road, they were.'

Deano paused in his story to let the words have their desired effect.

'Come on,' said somebody, at last. 'What did you do?'

'What do you think he did?'

It was Davey, the boy who had first noticed Mitch approaching, who spoke. Thin and unkempt, his complexion bad, he basked in Deano's reflected glory.

'He took off and flew over their heads.'

A stunned silence fell over the group, broken only by Deano's sudden laugh.

'Tell 'em what really happened, you jerk.'

Davey grinned.

'He braked hard. Christ, there was smoke coming off those tyres. The bloody car skidded all over the road and we ended up, arse end just three inches from the cop car. They thought we was going to hit them. You ain't ever seen two coppers so bloody frightened. Then we were off again, up the road before they could move.'

Deano reached over and caught Davey by the sleeve. Viciously, he pulled him close, hissing into his face through clenched teeth.

'That's enough. I'll take it from here. Don't want you stealing all my glory.'

Davey collapsed into sullen silence. He could not risk annoying Deano too much and accepted the humiliation with as much grace as he could muster.

'Speed,' said Deano, 'that's the key. And that's why we only take classy cars. Cars with a bit of poke. Golf GTIs, Cosworths. Even Astras, sometimes. Crap cars, tin boxes, that's all, but they go like hot snot!'

Mitch felt Deano's elbow nudge him in the ribs. The boy was winking at him, including him in the confidence. It felt good, exciting and dangerous but warm and secure as well. He suddenly felt as if he belonged.

'Are we on again for tonight?' asked Davey, the recent slight quickly forgotten.

Deano shrugged.

'As far as I'm concerned, yeah, why not? Who's coming?'

A shower of cries and calls echoed around the yard. Mitch felt Deano looking at him.

'What about you, kid?'

'Him?' sneered Davey. 'He's a bloody swot, a mummy's boy. He knows sod all about nicking cars. He's a chicken.'

Mitch felt anger and embarrassment clouding onto his face. He wanted to reach out and grab Davey, pull him close and quieten him with a hissed threat, just like Deano had done. But he knew he wouldn't do that, knew he wasn't yet brave enough. There was something he could do, though, to show he was not afraid.

'Yes,' he said. 'I'll come.'

He threw away the line casually, sounding a lot more confident than he felt.

'Good,' said Deano. 'That's five of us, then. Outside The Bird in Hand at nine o'clock. See you later.'

Peter had been puzzled when Mitch told him he would not be coming to the Chess Club that night.

'Why not?' he asked. 'We always go on a Tuesday night.'

'I've got something else to do, that's all.'

He walked away, leaving Peter staring after him. He couldn't tell Peter the truth, of course, he just wouldn't understand. And with his father being a policeman it would be decidedly dangerous. Keep him in the dark, Mitch decided, after all it was only for the one night. Tomorrow they would be the same again.

He spent the evening in his room, playing CDs. He had homework to do but decided, in a moment of rebellion, that it would remain untouched. Blow the homework, he thought, he probably wouldn't be able to concentrate on it anyway.

At eight-thirty he made an excuse, told his parents he had to see Peter about a history project and left the house before they had time to complain. A tense excitement burned at his insides. He was afraid but exultant at the same time.

When he reached The Bird in Hand Deano and the rest of them were waiting restlessly, hanging over and along the low wall that bordered the pub car park.

'Thought you weren't going to show,' Deano said, clapping his arm around Mitch's shoulders. 'Glad you're here.'

They prowled the streets of the town, full of noise and restless high spirits. At times, it seemed, noise was the most important element in the whole performance. If Deano, Davey or the others could make people stop and stare, make them shake their heads or complain with disapproval, then they were happy.

After a while, though, Mitch began to wonder. This was boring and was certainly not what he had imagined. It was all very well to kick over the odd dustbin or hurl obscenities at old people but he couldn't quite see what Deano and the rest got out of it.

'I thought we were going to steal a car,' he complained, amazed at his own forwardness.

They were standing on a street corner in the centre of town. Davey and one of the others were aimlessly kicking an empty coke can along the gutter. Deano looked totally bored.

'When the time's right, son,' he muttered. 'When the time is right.'

Ten minutes later, as they walked along a quiet back street, Davey came to a sudden halt. He glanced furtively at Deano and winked.

'XR3I. Other side of the road. The stupid bugger just got out and went indoors. He didn't lock the bloody thing.'

Deano glanced around, nodded and crossed the road. Carefully, he opened the driver's door, slipped into the seat and motioned the others to join him. There was a scrum of bodies and Mitch found himself in the centre of the back seat, his heart pounding frantically. They were off.

Deano rummaged around under the dashboard, pulling out wires and carefully matching them.

'Come on,' somebody muttered. 'He'll be back soon.'

'Don't rush me,' Deano drawled. 'Don't rush me.'

Presently the car coughed into life. The engine fired once, twice, then caught.

'Got it!' Deano laughed.

A fierce tug on the wheel and the steering wheel lock snapped off. Slamming the car into gear, Deano kicked the accelerator to the floor and they shot away in a spray of gravel and smoke. Glancing out through the back window, Mitch saw the car owner fly out of the door to his house and start up the road after them.

'Stop!' he screamed. 'Stop. That's my bloody car!'

'Piss off!' Davey called through the open passenger's window. 'Lock the bloody thing next time.'

Whatever else he might have been, there was no denying that Deano was a good driver. He threw the car around corners, gunned it down the straights and did handbrake turns on the dirt road outside the Youth Club. Clouds of dust rose like smoke into the air and dozens of girls poured out of the club to watch in admiration.

Mitch was full of mixed emotions. He had craved this type of attention for years. For the first time in his life people were staring at him, not as the class swot, but as somebody with power and vitality. And yet there was a vague sense of uneasiness as well, deep down inside. They were murdering this car, revving its guts out. Taking it was one thing, surely destroying it was quite another.

Twelve o'clock found them racing at a hundred and twenty down the motorway. It was the third time they had been down this stretch of road and Mitch was growing tired. He should have been home hours ago, his parents would be worried. He was bored with the banter and with the constant physical contact that seemed to pass as fun with these boys. Every joke or gibe was accompanied by a playful punch on the arm or by a sudden and painful neck lock. It was all beginning to get rather wearing.

'I think I'd better be heading home,' he announced as Deano slowed for the exit junction.

The others burst out laughing. Deano crabbed round in his seat.

'Home? Who the hell are you kidding? You're with us till the end, son.'

Mitch felt a pang of terror in his throat but said nothing. He was in it now and there was no way out.

'Hey, Deano, look at this.'

Davey had pulled open the glove compartment. Inside lay a small mobile telephone. Dean screeched to a halt and grabbed the phone. He grinned.

'You want some real fun? Watch this.'

His fingers swept over the keys, then he sat back in the seat.

'Police? Listen, you bastards, we've nicked a black XR3I. Five of us. We're at Junction 29. You want us, come and get us.'

He snapped off the phone and threw it back to Davey. His eyes were wild and excited.

'Now watch the buggers run.'

Davey giggled hysterically. Deano put the car in gear and pulled out into the traffic. Three times they circled the roundabout, the fear in Mitch growing by the second. Then, from the motorway below them, came the wail of a police siren. Off in the distance, a flashing blue light was growing closer and steadily closer.

'Here they come,' shouted Deano.

To the accompaniment of loud screams and laughter from the other boys, he booted the accelerator and the car tore down the other carriageway. One hundred and twenty, one hundred and thirty – the car could certainly move, Mitch decided. He was surprised to find himself still capable of rational thought, so vast and all-consuming was his fear. At this speed, however, Deano's control was not so sure and they swerved dangerously on several occasions.

'Christ, Deano, be careful,' Davey muttered, his face suddenly white and strained. 'You nearly had us over then.'

'Shut up! I'm driving.'

They tore up the slip road at the first exit. Still doing sixty, Deano shot across the Give Way, not even bothering to glance to his right.

'Look out!' Mitch screamed.

It was too late. The car had come from nowhere and caught them a glancing blow on the rear end. It was only the faintest of impacts but it was enough to swing their vehicle viciously around, spinning them like a child's top across the road, up onto the grass roundabout. Mud and grass sprayed twenty feet into the air as their wheels gouged huge ruts out of the earth. Davey screamed, his arms raised high across his face.

'Christ!'

The single expletive matched the explosion of the shattering windscreen. Ploughing into a huge concrete block, the car came to a sudden halt and Davey shot forward through the glass.

Silence fell, marred only by the laboured breathing of Deano, gasping and clutching at his ribs where the steering wheel had caught him. Davey lay, unmoving, at the front of the car, his blood already beginning to seep out onto the grass.

'Oh God,' somebody muttered. 'What happened?'

Mitch felt gingerly at the lump on his head and glanced back through the rear window. Two police cars had come to a halt behind them, their flashing lights tingeing the night with an unreal and nightmarish hue.

He thought bitterly and briefly about his narrow escape from death, then remembered Davey and shuddered. He thought about his parents and their shame. He thought about the police and retribution.

The fear, then, was so great, so totally consuming, that he was unable to think about anything. He realised, with a shock, that he was shivering, his legs thundering and shuddering in an uncontrollable spasm. A sudden wetness on his inner thigh brought him back to reality and he cried out in terror and in shame.

'Oh, God,' he whispered. 'What have I done?'

He glanced back at the police cars as one of the uniformed officers began to walk towards them. He carried a torch and his face was grim. The shuddering in Mitch's legs started again as, slowly, the policeman reached out for the door handle.

Activities and Discussion

When Mitch first sees Deano and his friends they are gathered together in a group. They are loud and yet appealing. Why is it that antisocial behaviours often seem attractive? The same thing could be asked about 'bad' characters in fiction. They always seem more interesting than 'good' ones – why do you remember Fagin but not Oliver Twist, why do you relate to Darth Vader but not Luke Skywalker or the shark Jaws but not the men who hunt him?

Why does Mitch agree to go out with Deano and his mates? Is he worried that they are going to do something criminal? What are the motives that drive him to join the boys in their car stealing enterprise?

Mitch makes the point that they are destroying the car by the way it is being driven. Yet he was part of the group that stole it in the first place. Is there a difference between the two crimes, stealing a car on the one hand, destroying it on the other? Why does Mitch see the one crime as being more serious than the other?

Why do you think Deano and his mates enjoy making a noise, making a nuisance of themselves? What do they gain from it? Is it any less delinquent than stealing a car? After all, it doesn't actually hurt anyone – it might annoy people but that's all. Or do you see it as antisocial behaviour that should be dealt with by the police?

What do you think will happen to Mitch, Deano and the rest of the boys at the end of the story? How will it affect Mitch who, up until now, has not had a criminal record and has never been involved with the police? What do you think Mitch's parents will say when they hear the news?

Writing

How do you think Mitch's friend Peter will react when he hears the news? Write one scene of a play that takes place in the school playground the morning after the crash. You need use only two characters, Mitch and Peter, but you can use more if you wish. Keep stage directions to a minimum.

Imagine that Mitch chooses to leave the group at the point where they are about to steal the car. Imagine, also, that the car does not crash. What will Deano and the rest say the next day, how will they treat Mitch? Tell the story.

You are a journalist on the local paper. Write an account of the incident, complete with headline and quotes from people like the car owner, the policemen involved and, possibly, one or two of the parents.

Young people are always being accused of antisocial behaviour. Why do you think this is? Write a page giving your views on the issue. Try and back it up with facts from the local paper or from the library.

Tell the story of a prank or piece of fun that goes terribly wrong – perhaps an accidental fire or a piece of silly behaviour that causes someone to get hurt.

Reflection

 ▸ Ask yourself if you have ever been tempted to carry out a criminal act. What stopped you?

 ▸ If you have actually done something illegal, ask yourself how you felt afterwards. How do you feel now? Are you likely to do something criminal again? If the answer is no, try to give your reasons for this decision.

CL

646.
700
835
CAR